Time Management

A Comprehensive Manual That Furnishes You With
Pioneering Methodologies And Strategies To Enhance
The Efficiency Of Your Endeavors

*(Acquire Proficiency In Time Management Techniques And
Gain Insights On Enhancing Efficiency)*

Sydney Castle

TABLE OF CONTENT

Enhance Your Time Management Skills Through The Practice Of Delegation And Outsourcing 1

The Significance Of Delegation And Automation - Achieving Success Demands Your Attention 12

The Individual Positioned On The Taut Wire, The Reptile Of The Crocodile Family, The Canine Predator, And The Infant Human Being 39

Get Started Already 58

Make Use Of Chances 85

We All Have The Same 24-Hours In A Day: Focus On What Matters 106

Time Management Training And Self-Discipline To Increase Your Productivity 108

Why Do You Put Off Things? 113

Time Management 125

15 Strategies That Will Enhance Your Workplace Productivity...163

I'm Not Sure Where To Begin. 193

Enhance Your Time Management Skills Through The Practice Of Delegation And Outsourcing

In the capacity of a business proprietor, it is incumbent upon you to oversee all facets of your enterprise, ranging from promotional endeavors to augmenting your customer base to ensuring exceptional client service and beyond. In order to allocate time for personal activities apart from your business, it is imperative to acquire the skill of delegating and outsourcing certain duties to highly competent professionals. Failure to do so will result in an overwhelming workload that will consume your time and energy. Entrepreneurs who attempt to handle all tasks single-handedly will ultimately succumb to exhaustion and ultimately experience downfall. Continuous work without breaks ultimately leads to a lack of concentration regarding strategies to enhance one's business and expand its clientele. Regrettably, attempting to manage all tasks independently can have detrimental effects on your business. Hence, it is imperative that you acquire the skill of task delegation in order to allocate your time more effectively towards the more crucial aspects of your business.

Mastering the Skill of Delegating

Acquiring the skill of effective delegation is not only a straightforward endeavor, but also exceedingly advantageous for the overall prosperity of your enterprise. The initial measure to be undertaken entails conducting an analysis and deliberating upon the assignment of your daily tasks, ascertaining the necessary actions to accomplish each task, establishing the expected standards for task execution and completion, and identifying the individuals most suitable for carrying out these tasks. It is imperative to ensure that the individual to whom you assign the task possesses the necessary skill set for its successful completion. If this is not the case, it is essential that they demonstrate the capacity to acquire the required skills through the process of learning. Prior to commencing the assignment of tasks, it is essential to reflect upon the following inquiries.

- Which tasks and activities have the potential to be assigned to others?

- What are the essential procedures required to accomplish the task?

- Which individual possesses the highest level of qualification to undertake the assigned task?

- Are they equipped with the necessary skills and resources to successfully accomplish the task in question?

a timely manner?

task? • Are they capable of handling the responsibilities associated with completing the task?"

task?

- What outcomes can I anticipate following the successful completion of the task?

In order to achieve success in delegation, it is imperative to thoroughly examine the process and invest ample time in strategic planning prior to proceeding. Numerous entrepreneurs tend to commit the error of assigning tasks without proper strategizing, a course of action that inevitably results in unfavorable outcomes. It is imperative that a sufficient amount of time be dedicated to carefully considering the process and formulating a strategic plan regarding the delegation of the task, including assigning the most suitable individual for the job and clearly articulating the desired outcome.

Another pivotal facet of delegation entails the capacity to communicate with clarity regarding your specific requirements, the designated timeframe for task completion, and the anticipated deliverables upon task conclusion. If there is a lack of clear understanding among those to whom you are assigning tasks, they will inevitably succumb to engaging in unproductive endeavors, thereby leading to a subsequent decline in motivation. Ensuring clarity in the explanation of tasks is of the utmost importance in order to achieve successful outcomes.

Delegating Tasks to Enhance Time Management Efficiency

Outsourcing is applicable not only to major corporations but also to smaller entities. Numerous small enterprises in the contemporary business landscape are capitalizing on the existing opportunity of outsourcing to enhance their business growth trajectory and optimize their proficiency in time management. Outsourcing enables the engagement of skilled professionals to handle tasks you lack the expertise or time to accomplish, while exempting you from the costs associated with training new staff or procuring necessary equipment for project execution.

The Benefits of Outsourcing the Work

The personnel within your organization represent both a substantial financial investment and a valuable resource. The collective factors of workforce size, skill repertoire, associated costs, and levels of drive and dedication collectively constitute the most pivotal determinants of your business's triumph or downfall. The ability to effectively allocate qualified individuals to the appropriate roles, precisely when required and at an optimal cost, confers a significant edge over rival entities.

The myriad advantages of outsourcing for your business are boundless. It enables you to allocate your attention towards strategic endeavors that propel your business growth. When the option to outsource job tasks is available, it frees individuals from the responsibility of grappling with the intricacies of assignments they may lack the requisite knowledge or skills to effectively accomplish. One may opt to delegate the task to an independent contractor or a specialized agency, specifically proficient in the respective field. This not only mitigates the likelihood of expensive errors, but it also produces heightened effectiveness, accelerated delivery, and an upsurge in productivity. Outsourcing has additionally demonstrated cost-effectiveness, leading to substantial savings and increased financial resources for your enterprise. By leveraging outsourcing, you can gain a distinct competitive advantage as it grants you additional time to focus on the more pivotal facets of your enterprise.

Categories of Tasks Suitable for Outsourcing

One can delegate a wide range of responsibilities, such as web services, administrative tasks, content creation, payroll, or any other tasks that are deemed more suitable for someone else to undertake. You may consider the option of outsourcing those tasks and projects that are repetitive and require extensive labor, but are essential for maintaining the seamless operation of your business. Presented below are a selection of tasks which you can delegate to optimize your time utilization and enhance your overall productivity.

- Data entry
- Editing
- Accounting tasks
- Budget management
- Website management
- Internet marketing
- Email management
- Order processing

- Customer service

The process of outsourcing and delegation offers a convenient and economically advantageous approach to increase productivity and achieve exemplary outcomes. Through the practice of delegation and outsourcing, individuals can reclaim their time and achieve greater productivity within a shortened timeframe.

The Significance Of Delegation And Automation - Achieving Success Demands Your Attention

In contemporary society, the prevailing norm is to undertake tasks independently. We have received instruction from our acquaintances and kinfolk that it is advisable, if one possesses the ability, to exercise frugality by conserving funds and addressing issues such as repairing a leaky faucet, mending a hole in the drywall, and rewiring the bathroom exhaust fan. One aspect that individuals frequently overlook is the element of time. Although it may come at a significant expense, hiring a professional plumber to address the issue with the faucet ensures that your wife can have confidence in the quality of the work. In addition, it is worth considering that the plumber will likely complete the task in a fraction of the time that it would have taken us, even up to three hours.

"Allow me to provide a personal illustration: After careful consideration, I opted to engage the services of a professional lawn care provider to consistently tend to the maintenance of my property on a weekly basis." This incurs an expense of $65 per week for me. My mother, who comes from a heritage that highly values savings, is diligently focused on economizing. She was greatly alarmed when she observed me expending such a substantial amount of funds on something I was fully capable of managing independently. Presently, my three gentlemen enter and, after a duration of 25 minutes, they and their high-quality machinery have vacated my meticulously maintained premises.

Considering the approximate duration of four hours, a comparable outcome could be achieved through the utilization of professional-grade equipment, such as a riding mower valued at $1,500, a blower priced at $200, and a weed whacker costing $150, not to mention the expense of procuring fuel (which I hesitate to quantify). By doing so, I would have managed to save $65. It appears utterly irrational, particularly considering my intentions to construct a new driveway and integrate a heating system into it.

According to my mother's statement, one can simply remove the excess snow as necessary and thus avoid incurring additional expenses.

Mother, the journey ahead is quite extensive. Now, the crux of the matter is that the time it would take me, or anyone else for that matter, four hours to mow the lawn or shovel the driveway could be utilized much more productively by engaging in other significant endeavors that actually generate income. As an illustration, I have opted to operate my own business from home.

So start delegating. Enlist the services of the carpenter to undertake the task of working on the kitchen cabinets, and observe the favorable financial outcomes resulting from enhanced productivity within the confines of your personal workspace. Encourage your children to responsibly attend to the car washing, or solicit the neighboring child's assistance in mowing the lawn if professional landscaping services are not feasible. Compensating them duly for their efforts will effectively instill the concept of acquiring personal income and understanding its significance. Discuss the concept of accomplishing multiple objectives simultaneously. The aforementioned examples are undoubtedly the most prevalent instances. It is advisable that you generate additional innovative illustrations on your own.

Please understand that if finding solace in mowing the yard serves as a therapeutic outlet for you, it is essential that you persist in pursuing this activity. However, I strongly discourage it for the purpose of achieving financial savings. In the long run, the expenses incurred will exceed the amount initially saved.

Delegation holds significant importance as a crucial skill within management.

These logical principles and methodologies will assist you in effectively assigning tasks. Effective delegation results in time savings, fosters the growth of individuals, cultivates potential successors, and serves as a source of motivation. Ineffectual delegation can engender frustration, undermine motivation, and engender confusion among others, ultimately resulting in the failure to accomplish the assigned task or purpose.

Delegating can be considered as a form of internal automation. The primary objective of delegation is to effectively manage one's time... In order to allow for your focus on significant matters... Primary tasks and assignments requiring your attention. However, it is crucial to determine what tasks can be assigned to others.

I firmly believe that individuals should refrain from delegating tasks beyond their own capabilities. This implies that one should only delegate those tasks and assignments in which they feel confident and competent. When delegating, the conveyed message to the recipient is one of acknowledging my ability to fulfill the task efficiently, but enlisting their assistance in completing this assignment so that I may allocate my focus to other matters or assignments.

It is possible that you have encountered or witnessed instances where supervisors delegate tasks that they themselves are unable to accomplish, resulting in the message being conveyed as, "I lack the ability to do it, and therefore, I require you to handle it."

So, now the paramount inquiry pertains to your proficiency in the practice of delegation?

The Correlation Between Automation and Delegation.

Automation refers to the act of transferring or delegating the operation and day-to-day management of a business process to an external service provider. The customer is provided with a service that fulfills a specific business function that aligns with the customer's overall business operations.

There exist two primary categories: "conventional" automation and "greenfield" automation.

In the realm of conventional automation, the workforce within an organization no longer assumes their previous roles for the enterprise. Alternatively, instead of identifying tasks that need to be performed, the service provider typically employs individuals to carry out these tasks.

In the context of greenfield automation, the enterprise undertakes modifications to its business processes without engaging in any form of personnel recruitment by the service provider.

The primary objectives of Delegation and/or Automation are:

Cut costs

Increase productivity

Enhance security and reliability.

Maximize uptime

Direct your focus towards fundamental capabilities

Delegation VS Empowerment

Delegation is a long-standing concept employed within the conventional management framework. The objective was to ensure parity in both responsibility and authority across all positions. When the process of delegation was executed appropriately, individuals were entrusted with the necessary authority to carry out their assigned tasks effectively. Drawbacks associated with this approach include the fact that conferring authority alone does not guarantee an individual's possession of the requisite skills, drive, and comprehension essential for effective performance.

Enabling individuals with decision-making authority and fostering their autonomy constitutes a fundamental principle within the emerging management framework. In the context of the modern adaptive organization, delegation is substituted with empowerment, and responsibility is supplanted by ownership. Establishing and assigning authority and responsibilities are essential components of organizational structure. They are predicated on characteristics of the organization rather than individual capacities. Empowerment and ownership are social dimensions of organizing, predicated on effectiveness and initiative, rather than solely on roles and obligations. They belong to people.

Now, proceeding with delegation.

Thus, do you possess a proficient ability in the art of delegation, or do you exhibit an even higher level of proficiency?

A succinct protocol for delegation is the commonly used acronym SMART, or even more appropriately, SMARTER. This is a concise checklist for effectively delegating tasks. Delegated tasks must be:

Specific

Measurable

Agreed

Realistic

Time bound

Ethical

Recorded

Conventional interpretations of the SMARTER acronym employ terms such as "Exciting" or "Enjoyable." However, while accomplishing a delegated task and receiving recognition for it can often lead to a heightened sense of motivation, which in itself can be stimulating and pleasurable, it is important to acknowledge that it is not always feasible to guarantee that all assigned work will genuinely be regarded as "exciting" or "enjoyable" by the recipient. Moreover, the 'Ethical' component is inherent to all our endeavors, provided that you adhere to this particular philosophy.

Strategies for Implementing Efficient Time Management in the Workplace

1) Familiarize yourself thoroughly with your objectives. Please feel free to approach your supervisor if you believe that the set objectives are impractical and cannot be sufficiently accomplished within the designated timeframe. It is advantageous to engage in early-stage

discussions rather than facing potential embarrassment in the future. Engage in assignments solely when you possess a high level of assurance.

2) Engaging in work-related discussions with your colleagues poses no adverse consequences whatsoever. It is not feasible to accomplish nearly all tasks independently. Allocate tasks among your colleagues. It is foolish to over burden yourself. It is imperative to distribute one's workload among others in order to complete assignments within the specified timeframe. Know your capabilities.

3) Establish proper organizational strategies for yourself. Exercise caution when handling your files, important documents, visiting cards, folders, and

other materials. Ensure that they are consistently organized in appropriate locations to avoid unnecessary time wasted on searching for them.

4) Demonstrate unwavering fidelity to your organization. Avoid working solely in the presence of your superiors. Please bear in mind that you are being compensated for your diligent efforts. Please direct your focus towards your assigned tasks instead of engaging in idle conversation or aimlessly lingering. Abstain from engaging in recreational computer gaming or engaging in endeavors that involve prying into the activities of your coworkers.

5) While it is acceptable to occasionally contact family members or friends, it is important to exercise caution and

refrain from engaging in lengthy telephone conversations during working hours. Telephone communications and electronic messages constitute significant disruptions in the workplace.

6) Make thorough preparations with ample lead time. Do not engage in work solely for the purpose of work itself. The initial action that an employee ought to undertake in the morning is to carefully document the various tasks that are to be accomplished throughout the entirety of the day, making sure to allocate specific time slots for each individual task. Creating a Task Plan at the commencement of the day consistently facilitates and endows one with a clear orientation in the workplace. A "list of tasks" indicates the course of action you should take. Tick off completed

assignments. Please ensure that you complete all assigned tasks within the designated timeframes.

7) Ensure that you have a notepad and pen readily available. Please refrain from documenting information on unsecured sheets of paper. One will invariably be unable to locate them at the time of actual necessity. It is advisable to utilize an organizer as it facilitates more effective planning of one's tasks.

8) Refrain from consuming meals outside of the designated lunch hours. Consuming food during the process of work not only induces drowsiness but also disrupts the flow of thought.

9) Be punctual. Minimize the frequency of absences from work unless they are necessitated by emergencies. Ensure

punctuality by consistently arriving to the office at the designated time.

10) It is imperative that you promptly address any outstanding matters. Promptly raise the issue that necessitates the endorsement of superior authorities. Please refrain from persistently disregarding matters. They will inevitably give rise to difficulties for you in due course.

Strategies for Effective Time Management in a Professional Setting:

A person who engages in unproductive activities while on duty is not well-liked by anyone and faces challenges in meeting deadlines effectively. He consistently fails to meet deadlines and frequently faces criticism from both colleagues and superiors for the quality of his work.

Allow us to examine several recommended Time Management strategies for professionals:

1) Ensure punctuality upon arrival at the office. Refrain from taking frequent absences from work. It is imperative to adhere to punctuality in order to effectively manage one's time. Please refrain from wandering aimlessly.

2) It is imperative for an employee to commence their day by crafting a meticulously detailed Task Plan. Please document the tasks that need to be completed within one day and allocate specific time intervals to each task based on their level of importance. Priority

should be given to urgent assignments, with low priority tasks to be addressed thereafter. Upon the successful completion of the task, mark it as accomplished. You will feel relieved.

3) Allocate a portion of your schedule for personal calls, engaging with acquaintances on social media platforms, posting updates on Twitter, or even reserving cinema tickets for leisure time.

4) Exhibit effective self-management. Ensure that your workstation remains clean and well-organized. It is imperative that the files and important documents are stored in their appropriate locations. Do not accumulate piles of files and excessive amounts of paper on the desk. Discard

any unnecessary items. Do not inscribe on unsecured documents, as it is highly likely that they will become misplaced or misplaced over time. Please ensure that all of your personal belongings are consolidated in a single location.

5) Please refrain from cluttering your desktop. Establish distinct directories to classify and arrange your paperwork. Please remove any unnecessary files and folders. Manage your emails well.

6) Employ a calendar or scheduling tool to efficiently allot and organize your daily activities. A tabletop calendar serves as a reliable tool for ensuring that important dates and meetings are never overlooked.

7) Depart slightly in advance for meetings held outside of the office.

Please allocate a sufficient amount of time to account for potential delays due to traffic congestion, alternative routes, or any unforeseen circumstances that may arise during your journey.

8) Establish a hierarchy of tasks for oneself. Do not undertake any assignment that you are aware to be challenging for you to successfully complete within the designated timeframe. Providing a resolute negative response from the outset will aid in preserving your reputation in the future.

9) Ensure clarity regarding your goals and objectives. It is imperative that the Key Result Areas (KRAs) of an employee are effectively and unambiguously conveyed to them. Know your targets. In the event that you perceive your

objectives to be unattainable, it is recommended that you promptly engage in communication with your supervising manager. Plan things well. Strategic planning facilitates the timely completion of tasks.

10) Refrain from engaging in idle chatter or lingering without purpose within the workplace. It has come to our attention that engaging in computer games during office hours is not a compensable activity in this department. Do not solely prioritize a paycheck or aim solely to satisfy your superiors. Work for yourself. The commitment should originate from an intrinsic source.

11) It is advisable to refrain from engaging in lengthy personal phone conversations during business hours.

Please bear in mind that completing your tasks within the designated timeframe will afford you the opportunity to allocate ample time for socializing with friends and family outside of working hours. Achieving a harmonious equilibrium between one's personal and professional commitments is imperative for sustained success in the future.

The Individual Positioned On The Taut Wire, The Reptile Of The Crocodile Family, The Canine Predator, And The Infant Human Being

Visualize an individual positioned on a taut wire, performing a balancing act. The taut wire stretches across an expansive chasm. The gentleman is not overly concerned as he possesses sound equilibrium and has traversed a tightrope on previous occasions. Subsequently, the gentleman directs his gaze towards the ground. Beneath him, situated within a profound water basin, resides a sizable alligator voraciously clamping its mandibles. The individual starts to perspire. As he directs his gaze upwards to fixate on the distant point, he cannot but ponder on the alligator lurking beneath, its jaws poised to snap. His heart starts to accelerate and he experiences slight unsteadiness while walking on the tightrope. At the precise moment prior to his undertaking of a subsequent stride, he perceives a low and ominous rumble emanating from his rear, thereby recognizing it as the presence of a wolf. He remains facing forward, yet while positioned on the taut rope, he unavoidably perceives the resounding echoes of ominous reverberations and the unsettling sound of grinding mandibles. The combination of the alligator's snapping, the threatening growl of the wolf, and the necessity of preserving his equilibrium gradually burden the man. As he contemplates the potential consequences of falling, the irreversible nature of the situation, and the imperative to maintain equilibrium, he experiences heightened distress. Shortly thereafter, the individual becomes immobilized, unable to advance further due to apprehension of plummeting, and retreat or surrendering is an impracticable course of action. At the very moment of relinquishing his hope completely, the man beholds an infant situated on the opposite end of the gorge. The infant is unaccompanied and moving swiftly towards the precipice of the ravine. Suddenly, the man begins to shuffle forward. Initially, his gait is unhurried, yet gradually he commences to encompass longer steps, ultimately traversing the canyon and securing the child in his embrace.

In the aforementioned narrative, the individual achieved success in traversing the canyon; however, what was the reason behind this accomplishment? And what were the reasons for his previous lack of success? While perched upon the taut tightrope, with limited mobility, he was filled with trepidation for his own well-being, as well as that of the child. However, he contemplated why, in one scenario, he possessed the ability to progress while remaining impeded in the other. The fundamental explanation lies in the ability of the human brain to engage in multitasking.

The Thing About Multitasking...

When we request the human brain to engage in multitasking, or allocate attention to multiple vital elements simultaneously, we are effectively splitting and distributing the cognitive resources at the brain's disposal. For instance, in the given scenario, the individual on the taut wire displayed unwavering concentration not solely towards traversing the gorge, but also directed his attention to the alligator positioned underneath him, and the wolf stealthily lurking in his wake. As he directed his focus towards these other matters, his ability to concentrate on traversing the tightrope safely diminished proportionally. On the other hand, however, when the man spotted the baby crawling to the edge of the canyon, his sole point of concentration was that baby. By directing his unwavering attention towards the infant, the gentleman successfully traversed the tightrope and rescued the child. Why? As there were no interruptions, no other demands depleting his scarce energy.

Therefore, how does this narrative pertain to you or any other subject, if at all? In the aforementioned instance, it can be observed that the more the man limited his points of focus, the greater his accomplishments and advancement.

The identical principle can be applied to routine office duties. Despite the assertions of certain individuals who profess to possess adept multitasking abilities, there exists a divergence of opinion among scientists on this matter. The capacity of the human brain to concentrate completely on a finite amount of information is restricted, and engaging in multitasking necessitates the brain to surpass this limit. Put simply, you are demanding that your mind concentrate on the wolf, the alligator, and maintaining your equilibrium. When such a occurrence takes place, the outcome is an absence of advancement. While it is unlikely that one would encounter the specific combination of a tightrope, an alligator, and a wolf simultaneously, the underlying concept of concentration remains relevant. Attempting to simultaneously engage in tasks such as finalizing a PowerPoint presentation, conducting discussions with your personal assistant regarding an upcoming meeting, and evaluating prospective candidates to fill a recently available position within your organization is an unreasonable demand on your cognitive faculties. To achieve advancement, it is imperative that you allocate your undivided attention to the primary undertaking at hand, namely the aforementioned project. Upon the successful completion of the aforementioned project, you shall have achieved one project successfully and shall subsequently be able to shift your attention towards the subsequent endeavor.

This appears to be a straightforward approach to facilitate advancement and effectively allocate time, thus why does it not function accordingly? The dilemma inherent in contemporary society lies in our collective persuasion that it is imperative to allocate our attention to multiple matters concurrently. Clearly, not in the guise of alligators and wolves, and not necessarily in the guise of multiple business endeavors. On how many occasions have you been present in a meeting wherein the sound of a cellular device interrupting the proceedings with its ringing has come to your attention? This phenomenon commonly serves as a source of distraction in our everyday routines. While we may remain oblivious to the presence of this disruption, it is diminishing our capacity to concentrate on the current objective. The division of attention rapidly fragments our focus, undermining both our concentration and overall productivity. It diverts our brain's attention towards the lurking alligator beneath, while simultaneously exerting efforts to compel it to concentrate on the current task despite the fact that merely half of its cognitive resources are available.

What is the significance of this matter? According to research findings, the human brain requires double the amount of time to regain focus on the primary task following an interruption or distraction. This implies that if you initially spent ten minutes commencing your PowerPoint presentation, it will require approximately twenty minutes to return to writing following an interruption. When accumulated over the course of the day, the combination of this twenty-minute interval and the duration dedicated to attending to other responsibilities significantly diminishes productivity in the workplace. This divergence from efficiency can be manifested in your capacity to complete a singular undertaking due to making minimal advancements on multiple projects, or it can be demonstrated in subpar output resulting from time constraints and lack of attention to detail due to divided focus.

Given that the brain lacks the capability to multitask, despite being consistently confronted with requests for multitasking, what measures can be undertaken to safeguard our focus from the distractions posed by these various demands?

Maintaining Control over the Beasts, Strategies for Enhancing Concentration

The distractions that hinder our focus inevitably lie in wait, necessitating a proactive stance to optimize our productivity. There are multiple approaches we can employ in order to achieve this outcome, such as intensifying our attention on core responsibilities and effectively blocking out potential sources of diversion. Now, let us examine the ways in which you can effectively execute these strategies.

Productivity Boosting Apps

A significant portion of the time that we squander on a daily basis is devoted to employing smartphones, tablets, and computers for activities such as checking email, making calls to friends, responding to texts, and engaging with applications. Considering the substantial amount of time we spend engrossed in technology, it would be prudent to transform our devices into instruments of efficiency and purpose rather than sources of diversion and disruption.

There exists a multitude of exceptional applications for smartphones, tablets, and desktops meticulously crafted to optimize business productivity. Although the apps we will disclose subsequently exhibit varying characteristics, they uniformly aspire to enhance concentration, focus, and overall business productivity. Allow us to examine the top five productivity applications.

1. Omnifocus enjoys widespread acclaim for its ability to enhance productivity, making it an app that comes highly recommended. Offered at no cost through a software application. In addition, the individual possesses professional expertise. In essence, Omnifocus offers a singular platform that encompasses every facet of life, while simultaneously safeguarding against any inadvertent overlap between

personal and professional matters. Supervise projects, stay abreast of assignments, effectively manage task lists, recall travel arrangements, and ascertain daily schedules prior to commencement.

2. RescueTime, a freemium application, has found application in numerous highly accomplished organizations. According to its assertions, the application purports to save nearly four hours of unproductive time per individual each week by allowing users to selectively restrict access to time-wasting websites. In addition, RescueTime offers a time tracking feature that enables users to gain insights into their daily allocation of unproductive time. This information can then be utilized to implement measures

that restrict access to websites that consume valuable time.

3. Wrike is a comprehensive project management solution offered both as a complimentary application and as a subscription-based service tailored to suit individual requirements. Wrike is a comprehensive solution that enhances time efficiency, concentration, and productivity by centralizing all pertinent project information in a single platform. Refrain from engaging in online activities that may cause distraction, as the Wrike platform is equipped with a comprehensive array of features including time tracking, workload management, task management, real-time news feed, seamless integration with popular services such as Dropbox and Google Drive, discussion

functionality, document collaboration services, as well as tailored reporting capabilities.

4. Introducing the Sound Curtain – Priced at $4.99, the Sound Curtain effectively enhances productivity within professional settings by employing a blend of white noise and harmonious sound. Using this application in conjunction with a headset effectively mitigates superfluous ambient noise in the workplace, thereby preventing potential distractions and promoting an optimal environment for accomplishing tasks.

5. Cue - A complimentary application, Cue may bear resemblance to a calendar and scheduling application. However, in reality, it surpasses or exceeds that

perception by a significant margin. Similar to your computer desktop, Cue efficiently organizes and integrates all of your network accounts, social media accounts, e-mail accounts, Dropbox account, Airline network information, and your calendar. Regard it as a personalized organizational tool to efficiently manage and address your distractions in a consolidated manner.

Get Started Already

Now that you have familiarized yourself with the 8 principles that will facilitate the attainment of the desired outcomes, it is imperative that you employ this knowledge. Subsequently, the subsequent course of action involves the practical implementation of these principles. Perhaps you could commence by implementing a solitary minor alteration, or alternatively, immerse yourself fully and undertake a comprehensive overhaul of your entire existence. You possess the requisite knowledge and abilities to attain all your aspirations; the responsibility to seize these opportunities now rests solely on your shoulders.

Ensure timely action in the pursuit of manifesting your ideal life. Please ensure to maintain your concentration, derive lessons from any errors, and incessantly pursue enhancement. Please record your daily objectives and ensure that you have a clear understanding of the reasons behind your drive to achieve them. When embarking upon the pursuit of these objectives, it is advisable to employ diverse strategies and embrace the prospect of committing errors without hesitation. At the conclusion of each day, engage in a retrospective analysis of your achievements and outstanding tasks. Envision ambitious goals and seek the guidance of compatible individuals who can serve as your mentors throughout your journey.

The moral that this narrative imparts

We have collectively encountered occurrences of this nature throughout the course of our existence. This narrative revolved around the unfortunate occurrence of not securing my desired professional opportunity. I am confident that you have encountered similar situations in your professional endeavors, personal relationships, or various facets of your life. In such circumstances, it is not uncommon for us to label ourselves as individuals prone to procrastination and assume responsibility for our actions. The fact remains that we all evade issues; it is inherent in our genetic makeup to delay action when faced with particular circumstances. I do not intend to imply that this book is solely meant for procrastinators, however, it is essential that we address this topic first if you desire to effectuate that transformation. In this chapter, I shall present an analysis of the underlying factors that frequently lead to procrastination, thereby imparting a comprehensive understanding to readers. Upon experiencing a comparable circumstance to that of my job application, you will gain comprehension regarding the factors impeding your progress, thereby facilitating the identification of viable solutions.

I employ the sport of soccer as a means of drawing parallels and making comparisons to our predetermined fate. I regrettably failed to capitalize on a significant opportunity by not successfully directing the ball into the net, whereas another individual seized the moment and successfully scored the goal. This book emphasizes the importance of seizing opportunities as they arise. I refrain from making a sweeping statement encompassing all possibilities as not every opportunity may effectively contribute to the achievement of your objectives. However, when it comes to significant opportunities in life, this book is designed to help you seize those moments promptly and avoid any future remorse. This book aims to assist you in becoming a proficient clinical striker with a keen ability to score goals.

What are the Benefits of Listening to Someone Who Has Overcome Procrastination as a Former Practitioner?

What makes me the appropriate individual to lend an ear to? As I reflected upon my past actions, it became evident to me that I might have held the distinct title of being the most severe procrastinator known to mankind, or so I believed. Previously, I grappled with procrastination, which hindered my drive and determination to actively pursue my aspirations and long-term objectives. Truly, procrastination lacks rationale. It is generally more expedient to promptly complete a task rather than procrastinating until the final moments. Within the realm of our logical minds, we collectively acknowledge that evading action typically yields unfavorable outcomes. However, our complex cognitive capacities as humans refuse to acknowledge such notions, consequently exerting dominance over our mental processes and behaviors.

I overcame my tendency to procrastinate by implementing well-structured systems and cultivating disciplined habits. To put it differently, cultivating self-discipline. But what I am going to share with you is why we always fall into this procrastination trap no matter how pumped up or activated we feel. However, it is important to note that there exist two distinct types of procrastination.

Active vs. Passive Procrastination

It is conceivable that you may be astounded by the existence of two distinct types of procrastination. Are there multiple things to fixate on? Both categories impede our progress and hinder us from attaining our objectives. However, our mindset does not align precisely with this perspective. In a formal tone, one could say: "Active procrastination entails a deliberate approach in which an individual intentionally defers a task until the deadline or last moment, as they perceive that they perform more effectively under pressure." This was precisely the underlying motive behind my deliberate decision to postpone my projects until they were closer to the deadline. I held the conviction in Parkinson's Law, a topic that shall be further discussed in subsequent sections of this chapter. When I was facing demanding circumstances, I became even more motivated. Consistently, I provided clients with high-quality work for the majority of the projects.

Hastening or expediting tasks is not conducive to well-being, however, active procrastinators adeptly employ their own approach to ensure its efficient execution.

Suppose I were assigned a project, such as the task of composing and designing a company brochure on behalf of a client, which necessitates a minimum of 12 meticulously crafted pages. Under these circumstances, the client has granted me a week to finalize the task. An individual who possesses excellent organizational skills would allocate several hours each day to diligently work on the project, resulting in its timely completion well before the end of the week. Proponents of active procrastination intentionally postpone tasks until the eleventh hour. This does not imply that they will have only one day remaining to write all 12 pages. In this particular instance, I would propose allocating one page on the initial day, followed by an additional three pages on the fourth day. With a mere two days remaining, I would intentionally reserve eight pages, as I tend to feel more motivated and productive when the deadline draws near. Naturally, acquiring mastery in this endeavor necessitates consistent practice and a comprehensive comprehension of the intricacies inherent in the project. Active procrastinators exhibit proficiency in that aspect. Engaging in deliberate delay could be perceived as beneficial when one is juggling multiple tasks and aims to prioritize completing a particular project nearer to its deadline. Nonetheless, this does not imply that this is the exemplar you should aspire to emulate. If you possess the characteristic of being an engaged procrastinator, it is likely that you derived pleasure from perusing that segment and obtaining a deeper comprehension of your own disposition.

Conversely, passive procrastinators refrain from intentionally delaying tasks to the final moment. Typically, individuals tend to postpone such matters until the eleventh hour due to the overpowering influence of adverse emotions. There may exist concerns relating to self-assurance, anxiety, and similar matters. The task at hand can pose a significant challenge, potentially resulting in failure if one becomes inundated with its demands. Ultimately, doubting yourself. Passive procrastinators are individuals with whom we often find ourselves associating. We must make every effort to steer clear of this form of procrastination, as it is counterproductive and detrimental to the achievement of our objectives. If you desire to delve into the underlying reasons behind your propensity for frequent passivity on the procrastination spectrum, let us explore prevalent challenges and ascertain if you can identify with them.

Unveiling the Reasons Behind Procrastination

Now, I shall proceed to elucidate several rationales for our propensity to procrastinate and ultimately veer away from our aspirations. Conversely, we dedicate valuable time towards unproductive activities solely for the sake of experiencing a dopamine surge, ultimately leading to remorseful outcomes. Once you have comprehended these rationales, you will be adequately equipped to confront any circumstance, as you possess a deep understanding of the underlying verity that hinders your progress.

Fear of Failure

Have you ever deferred tasks due to the fear of potential failure? You exhibited a strong desire for success, to the extent that you consciously evaded undertaking this task in order to prevent the possibility of failure. If you refrain from making an effort, you will not experience failure. Certainly, we ought not to adopt such a mindset when undertaking a specific task or project. I comprehend your apprehension regarding the potential mismatch between your work and the client's expectations, which could potentially be perceived as a failure. However, consider the situation from an alternate perspective. Your failure was evident as soon as you chose not to make an effort and withdrew from the competition. One can derive valuable lessons from failure when they strive to do their utmost, accepting their imperfections along the way.

I am not suggesting or advocating for you to actively engage in endeavors that are likely to result in failure. It is imperative that you tackle each task with an attitude that encompasses the absence of fear or concern about potential consequences. Inevitably, when you undertake a task, there will eventually come a point at which you experience failure. One can derive lessons from past misfortunes and emerge stronger. Adversity can serve as a valuable instructor when we acquire the skills to extract wisdom from these experiences and rise resiliently. Whenever you find yourself confronted with a blank document or experiencing hesitation in making a call to finalize a deal, it would be judicious to consider taking action rather than deliberating further. Throughout the course of your work, you are encouraged to periodically reassess areas in which you believe there is room for improvement and make iterative adjustments accordingly.

The Characterization of the Undertaking

Do you perceive the task as arduous or monotonous? Does your project inundate you with an excessive amount of intricate particulars? It is quite normal to experience such emotions. You need to consider whether you find this task overly monotonous or if you are having difficulty comprehending the entirety of this particular project on your own. There exist two approaches to address the intricacy of the tasks that we are currently facing. An alternative approach would be to refrain from perceiving your project as a single overarching phenomenon. When one engages in visualization, particularly of a substantial nature, it has the potential to evoke intimidation. In future instances where you embark on a sizable endeavor, it would be advisable to fragment the undertaking into more manageable components. If the objective entails executing interior design for the client's workplace, it is advisable to subdivide the project into more manageable and easily comprehensible tasks. Create a comprehensive list and mark off the following tasks: painting the office walls, repairing the flooring, importing office furniture, installing the necessary fixtures, and adding the final touches with office embellishments.

It is evident what I am attempting to accomplish in this context. By subdividing your substantial undertaking into smaller, attainable objectives, the work becomes more manageable and the perceived intimidation of the tasks at hand diminishes. An alternative approach to engender a sense of gratification from a mundane task is to imbue it with aspects that stimulate interest. Devise your schedule in a manner that fosters personal satisfaction in carrying out these tasks. Perhaps you could consider pushing yourself to accomplish a portion of this task within a designated timeframe, as a means to earn a well-deserved reward of your choosing. Alternatively, you can enhance the purposefulness of your task by establishing a system in which an accountability partner regularly monitors your progress. Implementing strategies that ensure the timely completion of laborious tasks will effectively eradicate tendencies for procrastination and facilitate prompt initiation of projects. In essence, seek avenues for streamlining arduous and monotonous tasks, rendering them more effortless and pleasurable.

Being a Perfectionist

On occasion, I find myself culpable of displaying perfectionistic tendencies. I have a strong preoccupation with ensuring exceptional quality. If you happen to share this sentiment, you will realize that it may not necessarily be an unfavorable quandary to encounter. Silver medals are not desired by anyone. We are all eager to acquire the golden ones. Ultimately, our objective is to produce work of impeccable quality in order to fulfill our own standards and meet the expectations of others. However, when the pursuit of perfectionism begins to have adverse effects on one's performance, leading to procrastination, it becomes imperative that we steer clear of such tendencies.

Indeed, we are not devoid of imperfections. No one is. We are prone to err on occasion, yet the objective is to minimize the occurrence of errors. An effective approach to combating this sensation is to initially acknowledge the inherent imperfections in everything. Subsequently, adopt a mindset centered around adhering to minimal standards to address the issue of procrastination and initiate your project. The problem at hand is our tendency to expend excessive time contemplating methods to achieve exceptional visual presentation, resulting in a failure to initiate work on the project. However, consider the alternative perspective. Rather than focusing solely on achieving perfection in your work, strive to ensure that your project meets a satisfactory standard, or at the very least, is not the least favorable among its peers. One can gain a comprehensive understanding by thoroughly analyzing the factors contributing to the substandard quality of one's work. As a result, you will minimize errors and meet or exceed minimum standards, thus, fulfilling your task. I can identify with this sentiment as I often find myself contemplating the completion of a singular task, focusing on the execution of the work and delivering a satisfactory level of effort. In due course, I ultimately surpassed both my client's and my own anticipations. Eliminate a perfectionist mindset and seek to do your work positively without worrying about being outstanding.

Lack of Self-Control

The absence of self-discipline can arise as a result of a multitude of factors. It is possible that you possess limited understanding or expertise regarding a specific project. This has the potential to result in diminished self-confidence and facilitate the domination of procrastination. One might underestimate the project's timeline and possess a misguided sense of assurance due to a lack of comprehensive understanding. Upon uncovering the veracity, one may find oneself inclined to engage in procrastination.

Maintaining mastery over your tasks is consistently imperative in order to dictate the course of your own future. How do you handle these situations?

One method involves giving priority to your tasks. By prioritizing them according to their significance, you will demonstrate a heightened sense of urgency to commence work on them without delay. Create lists of tasks and strategize the management of your responsibilities. Further information on these techniques will be presented in the subsequent chapters. Instead of underestimating the timeframe, consistently err on the side of caution by overestimating it. Undoubtedly, you will inevitably demonstrate a greater sense of urgency, ultimately ensuring the timely completion of the project with ample time remaining.

Distractions Everywhere

An alternate explanation for procrastination may not have any relation to your own actions. Frequently, it is the encompassing milieu that influences one's surroundings, including the impact of social media, indulgent confections, idle chatter, auditory disruptions, atmospheric conditions (though seemingly trivial, they can indeed be distracting), and so forth. In our present times, we inhabit a society that is constantly surrounded by numerous distractions and fortunate to possess an abundance of technological devices. Nevertheless, these entities have the potential to serve as diversions, fostering lethargy and consuming greater amounts of time. Ultimately, one tends to engage in procrastination, thus failing to achieve their intended goals. In order to address such circumstances, it is imperative that you strategize the structure of your surroundings to effectively minimize any potential distractions. We will engage in a comprehensive discussion regarding the elimination of distractions in Chapter 7. So, next time you blame yourself for procrastinating, look around you first and see what is taking your attention.

Parkinson's Law

I strongly adhere to the notion that Parkinson's Law governs my inclination towards active procrastination, resulting in a substantial workload accumulated within a constrained time period. Parkinson's Law posits that the scope of work enlarges in correspondence with the available timeframe designated for its accomplishment. This concept was derived from one of Cyril Northcote Parkinson's literary works in the year 1955. In the event that you are assigned a project that ideally has a one-day duration but are allocated a period of three days to accomplish it, his perspective suggests that you would utilize the entirety of the allotted three-day timeframe for its completion. If provided with a 24-hour time frame, you would be able to accomplish the task within that allotted period. The allocated time holds minimal significance, as evident.

Parkinson's Law can elucidate the extent to which you tend to procrastinate on your tasks. In accordance with this principle, you may choose to exhibit a sense of urgency at a later stage, as the completion deadline draws near. On certain occasions, this can facilitate effective performance in high-stress situations, albeit there is potential for adverse outcomes. In order to address such circumstances and mitigate dependence on working under pressure, I would propose the implementation of incentives to encourage the timely completion of tasks. When you complete a task early, reward yourself. An additional valuable suggestion is to establish an artificial time limit well in advance of the designated completion date. If you strive to accomplish the task within the designated timeframe, you will have ample opportunity to enhance the overall quality of the deliverable at a later stage.

Make Use Of Chances

Numerous opportunities go unnoticed each day due to insufficient thoughtful consideration by individuals. In the event of an illness-related absence, one is required to subsequently make up for the missed work; however, embracing timely opportunities might mitigate the perceived adverse consequences to a significant extent.

Acquire fresh knowledge.

In an occupational pursuit, acquiring fresh knowledge will facilitate your progression towards your desired trajectory. Therefore, cautiously evaluate the available prospects within your organization in order to propel your professional trajectory. It is conceivable that your employer may grant you the opportunity to utilize paid leave in order to acquire those supplementary credentials. It is possible that your company might be willing to provide financial support for your educational pursuits.

Provide instruction on a novel concept.

In the professional setting, exhibit willingness to impart your expertise to colleagues. Develop the practice of frequently engaging in training sessions. Providing colleagues with appropriate training in tasks that are integral to your role can ultimately yield substantial time savings, subsequently affording these colleagues a valuable opportunity for professional growth. Moreover, it facilitates the development of more amicable relationships with colleagues. Instructing others facilitates the development of a proactive and extroverted disposition. The magnitude of the task holds no relevance. Establish a routine of instructing an individual on a novel task on a daily basis. It would be feasible to arrange a designated time for training. This can also be applicable within a domestic setting. If your child possesses the knowledge and ability to engage in the task of cleaning your vehicle, it would be prudent to permit them to undertake said responsibility in exchange for additional financial compensation. Should your child possess the ability to paint walls, it shall serve to assist you in conserving valuable time. Engage in knowledge dissemination, distribute collective responsibilities, and enhance the quality of life.

Do not hesitate to acquire knowledge.

Developing the practice of acquiring new knowledge will contribute to the stimulation of your cognitive faculties. Utilize periods of available time during which you are not occupied with any other tasks. For instance, if one is aware of the likelihood of encountering traffic while commuting to work, why not seize this chance to acquire a new language or engage in listening to an enlightening CD imparted by a mentor? This period of time does not necessarily need to be devoid of productivity.

Develop the practice of declining offers or requests

You might question the manner in which this will enhance your prospects, however, it undoubtedly does so. If you continuously allocate your time to attending to individuals who habitually exploit your assistance, it becomes increasingly challenging to allocate time towards pursuing your own endeavors productively. Therefore, in the event that you perceive yourself being treated as a doormat, firmly assert yourself by emphatically declining and demonstrating utmost sincerity in your refusal. It would significantly reduce the amount of time available for engaging in other tasks of greater value and benefit.

Allocate some time for yourself.

Often, individuals encounter occasions in their lives where they have the chance to indulge in personal solitude, yet they tend to abstain due to the perception of selfishness associated with it. Alter your perspective regarding this matter, as incorporating dedicated personal time renders you more resilient and consequently enables you to maintain a positive demeanor when interacting with others or within professional settings, free from the intrusion of negative emotions that could diminish your motivation. Similar to the benefits of taking breaks from your workstation during the day, it is equally crucial to allocate a dedicated area in your residence for personal endeavors. There exists an excellent system that is designed to assist individuals within the professional setting. By utilizing a timer to allocate 25 minutes for focused work, succeeded by a ten-minute respite away from your workspace, you will enhance your productivity level. The rationale behind this practice stems from the fact that allocating some dedicated time for personal rejuvenation allows you to replenish your energy reserves. Consequently, upon returning to your workstation, you are able to enhance your level of productivity.

Maintain a harmonious equilibrium between your personal and professional spheres

This practice is instrumental in achieving a state of equilibrium in one's life. Produce a visual depiction of a set of weighing scales. When documenting your work tasks, record them on a designated page. Please record home-related tasks on the reverse side when performing them. Acquire the skill to modify your habits in cases where one side is overwhelmed and the other is vacant. You must strive for a harmonious equilibrium between your professional and personal lives, as it is crucial for one's overall well-being and achievement in life. Prominent entrepreneurs assert that achieving a harmonious equilibrium between one's personal and professional life is indispensable for attaining success.

Develop the ability to have faith in your instincts.

In the present era, individuals exhibit a decreased reliance on intuition. The cacophony of the world often drowns out its own existence, rendering it unheard to our senses. Seeking moments of tranquility can be beneficial, but it would also be advantageous to carry a notebook for the purpose of jotting down important information that may require future reference. When confronted with a choice, inquire within to ascertain your instinctive response. Place greater trust in your own judgement and endeavor to disregard the distractions of life, instead prioritizing the consideration of rational solutions derived from within yourself.

Opportunities lie in store for you in your journey, and if you find yourself occupied with other pursuits, there is a likelihood that these opportunities shall elude you. Hence, it is advisable to cultivate the behaviors outlined in this chapter, as they will assist you in identifying promising opportunities that may arise, rather than allowing them to slip away unnoticed.

If achieving inner stillness proves challenging, consider allocating a minimum of ten minutes each day to solitude, finding a quiet spot away from others. During this time, engage in deep, conscious breathing, ensuring that thoughts do not intrude upon your thoughtscape. This will aid in decluttering your thoughts, facilitating discernment and promoting sensible decision-making. I have elected to reserve the final habit for the purpose of conclusion, as it holds significant importance. If you initiate its usage, you will discover the unlocking of latent capabilities and a reduction in the time allocated to indulging in procrastination.

Disparity Between Intention and Action

There exists a multitude of permutations of procrastinators. Over the course of extensive research conducted over the years, several overarching observations have emerged. The individual with a persistent habit of procrastination consistently encounters difficulties when it comes to completing tasks, whereas individuals who engage in circumstantial procrastination frequently delay the progress of tasks based on the specific circumstances surrounding them. The most adverse confluence occurs when an individual possessing deficient self-discipline and heightened impulsivity encounters a disagreeable undertaking. The majority of individuals who procrastinate exhibit behavior that undermines their own success due to factors such as perfectionism or a fear of failure. However, it can also arise from a positive perspective, such as the exhilaration associated with the allure of temptation. This is the explanation behind why numerous researchers allude to procrastination as the "paragon" of self-control failure.

Individuals exhibiting pronounced impulsivity, a deficiency in discipline and self-control, are prone to observe a greater propensity for procrastination in comparison to those who have cultivated their capacity for self-control. Typically, individuals exhibit a certain level of ego regulation when they defer or postpone taking on responsibilities. Subsequently, they will proceed to offer justifications for their tardiness. These rationales fulfill a crucial function. They afford individuals the opportunity to persist in their procrastination habits, as they downplay the repercussions stemming from their actions, and allow them to cultivate a sense of self-satisfaction.

Social scientists, however, have engaged in discourse regarding whether this disparity can be characterized as a deficiency in time management skills or a lack of emotional and mood regulation proficiency. Numerous individuals adhere to the elucidation of procrastination as expounded upon in the 2007 publication of the Psychological Bulletin authored by Piers Steel, an esteemed professor from the University of Calgary. According to his conception, the procrastinator considers the degree of enjoyment associated with various activities. The items that provide greater enjoyment possess enhanced worth, whereas challenging tasks gain value as their deadline approaches.

Conversely, psychologists such as Pychyl and Ferrari recognize the limitations inherent in this temporal perspective. For instance, in the case where the delay is considered to be a rational thought according to this perspective, the term procrastination would not be necessary to describe this conduct. It would be more precise to designate it as time management. Furthermore, numerous studies have yielded findings indicating that individuals who exhibit procrastination tendencies also experience emotions such as guilt, anxiety, or shame as a result of their decision to delay taking action. This affective element indicates that there is a deeper narrative beyond mere temporal organization. Pychyl initially commenced his investigation into the correlation between emotions and mood with regards to procrastination in the 1990s. He subsequently substantiated his hypothesis by publishing his study in the renowned Journal of Social Behavior and Personality in the year 2000. In his research, he enlisted a group of forty-five undergraduate students to carry a pager at all times, and closely observed their activities for a period of five days preceding a significantly crucial examination. The participants were signaled eight times per day, and on each occasion, they recorded their level of procrastination and emotional disposition. As the difficulty and pressure of their test preparation intensified, the students would procrastinate on them in favor of more gratifying activities. Upon performing this action, they also exhibited a heightened sense of culpability, thus indicating that they retained residual apprehension towards the significant task that they had neglected. Pychyl's findings indicated that individuals who engage in procrastination are not oblivious to the negative consequences of their behavior, rather, they experience a compelling emotional desire for diversion that they struggle to resist.

An additional research article, which was published in the reputable Journal of Personality and Social Psychology in 2001, further supported the significance of mood in this context. Tice and his team discovered that students would refrain from procrastination prior to a significant evaluation if they were informed that their mood would remain constant. However, upon considering the possibility of a shift in their mindset, they deferred the task of studying until the final moments. His research findings indicated that an individual's self-regulation would only deteriorate when they believed that their emotional state could be enhanced.

As a general rule, individuals acquire knowledge from their errors, prompting them to adopt alternative strategies when facing challenges. In regards to individuals who habitually procrastinate, this perspective proves to be ineffective. This issue hinders their recognition of the necessity to initiate their work at an earlier stage. The elucidation of this behavior resides in the emotional realm of procrastination. Paradoxically, the urge to alleviate stress in the moment prompts a procrastinator to contemplate potential solutions for resolving this issue.

Several years ago, Fuschia Sirois assembled a cohort of eighty students to partake in an investigation, whereby their inclination towards procrastination was meticulously assessed. The participants perused accounts of challenging circumstances brought about by avoidable procrastination. In one of the given scenarios, an individual returned from their holiday to discover the presence of a mole that appeared suspicious. However, they failed to promptly seek medical attention, resulting in a distressing predicament.

Subsequently, Sirois sought the participants' perspectives on the given situation. The observation was made that individuals in the group who tend to procrastinate articulated sentiments such as, "At least they sought medical attention prior to the situation worsening." This phenomenon is commonly referred to as a downward counterfactual, indicating a desire for immediate enhancement of one's emotional well-being. Moreover, individuals exhibiting these tendencies scarcely expressed sentiments akin to "Had they only taken action earlier." This type of thinking, known as an upward counterfactual, highlights the inherent conflict within a particular situation, compelling one to seek meaningful insights. Essentially, individuals who procrastinate tend to prioritize finding ways to alleviate their negative emotions stemming from unpleasant memories.

Pychyl and Sirois endeavored to integrate the affective and temporal dimensions of procrastination in their recent study. In a publication of Social and Personality Psychology Compass, they presented a dualistic hypothesis regarding procrastination, whereby they established a linkage between immediate mood enhancements and the subsequent development of long-term temporal difficulties. The notion holds that individuals who engage in procrastination seek immediate solace while simultaneously relying on misguided beliefs that they will be psychologically equipped in the future.

We All Have The Same 24-Hours In A Day: Focus On What Matters

How about implementing a 48-Hour Productivity system within the confines of a 24-hour day? There are myriad tasks to accomplish within the limited timeframe available, correct? Wrong!

Effective time management entails optimizing productivity through strategic work methods, rather than solely relying on excessive effort.

Effective time management, unwavering focus, and intrinsic drive form the bedrock of strategizing and attaining our objectives, subsequently enhancing our overall productivity. Diversion can transform ostensibly eventful days into unproductive periods, engendering an adverse influence on our efficiency.

It appears that the allocation of time within a day is consistently insufficient. However, considering that everyone is allocated the same 24 hours, why is it that certain individuals achieve a higher level of productivity within the same timeframe?

The solution lies in the optimization of one's efforts rather than solely relying on sheer exertion.

The individuals who achieve the highest levels of success are adept at effectively managing their time.

One must simply acquire proficiency in time management and goal setting methodologies to concentrate on what truly holds significance, emphasizing those endeavors that bring us closer to realizing our immediate and future objectives, thereby enabling the fulfillment of our existence.

Engaging in a multitude of tasks does not necessarily equate to being productive.

The primary aim is to accomplish a greater volume of work within a reduced timeframe.

How? Establish your objectives, strategically execute essential tasks to optimize outcomes, reduce stress levels, and enhance various facets of your existence.

Time Management Training And Self-Discipline To Increase Your Productivity

The attainment of objectives and the optimization of outcomes over an extended period depend heavily on the cultivation and exercise of self-discipline.

To establish enduring success, it is imperative to consistently dedicate oneself to pursuing goals on a daily basis, rather than sporadically.

Cultivating self-discipline can be a challenging endeavor; however, it bestows numerous advantages upon one's life.

What factors contribute to enhancing one's self-discipline?

Motivation. The implementation of target setting and deadline establishment can serve as highly effective strategies for boosting motivation and enhancing outcomes, while simultaneously upholding a harmonious equilibrium between work and personal life. Increased motivation corresponds to a higher level of self-discipline.

The scientific principles underlying the enhancement of motivation are straightforward. It is possible that you are acquainted with the term "dopamine" as it relates to the neurology of humans. It is a substance that is emitted by neuronal cells.

(neurons) to transmit signals to adjacent neurons. The cerebral cortex consists of multiple dopamine pathways, with one in particular being heavily involved in the motivational aspect of behavior driven by rewards.

The human brain possesses the remarkable ability to adapt and modify itself to acquire novel habits and behaviors. Thus, it is crucial to furnish the mind with appropriate cognitive stimuli in order to effectively train it.

You will direct your attention towards crucial priorities and establish a productive regimen.

Each Achievement Commences with the Determination to Attempt.

The more promptly you initiate action, the greater the probability of commencing your efforts towards accomplishing your objective.

The higher your level of motivation, the greater your determination in pursuing optimal outcomes.

To enhance one's self-discipline, it is advisable to bolster motivation, eradicate procrastination, and initiate a shift in habits towards the attainment of goals. This can be achieved by cultivating a growth mindset that fosters success.

Why Do You Put Off Things?

Every individual harbors varying motivations behind the action of procrastination. In the forthcoming chapter, we shall delve into the pursuit of unraveling the specific factors that fuel your tendency to procrastinate. Indeed, as individuals, we seldom engage in any action unless there is a discernible gain or advantage to be obtained from it. One of the primary factors contributing to individuals' tendency to procrastinate is the perception that the task at hand will be monotonous or lacking in interest. Frequently, we perceive tasks as time-consuming and tedious, ultimately setting ourselves up for failure.

7. Change your mindset. If one commences a task with the anticipation of it being tedious or prolonged, that is precisely how it shall transpire. It is imperative that you alter your cognitive approach towards the task at hand. Consider the following perspective: When faced with a task that aligns with my interests and brings me enjoyment, commencing the undertaking requires no external motivation. I expedite the task efficiently due to my anticipation of deriving pleasure from it. In the past, when faced with employment opportunities that did not pique my interest, I would procrastinate before commencing the tasks, subsequently succumbing to distractions. Having acquired this knowledge, I am now aware of the urgency to commence the task promptly and complete it

expeditiously. I am aware that by completing the task expeditiously, I will experience a heightened sense of satisfaction and alleviate any anticipatory anxiety associated with that particular assignment. The focus primarily revolved around altering my mindset regarding the task at hand.

Another factor contributing to procrastination is a lack of organizational skills or, alternatively, a tendency to forget about one's obligations to complete a particular task. This is an additional factor that highlights the significance of maintaining a notebook. In the event that one finds oneself in a state of idle contemplation, devoid of specific tasks to pursue, one may promptly consult their notebook as a means of recollecting the pending duties. This holds significant importance for individuals who are engaged in remote work. Frequently, one may find themselves accepting assignments, yet despite acknowledging the need to complete them, they may instead occupy themselves with alternative responsibilities. Subsequently, your client might question the reasons behind the unfinished completion of the task. It is imperative that you diligently document all the tasks you must accomplish to ensure nothing is overlooked. It is unrealistic to anticipate being able to remember and fulfill all of your responsibilities on a daily basis.

Individuals often exhibit a tendency to defer tasks due to feelings of insecurity, self-doubt, or apprehension regarding potential failure. This is the point where you will need to invest effort in personal growth and self-improvement.

8. Comprehend the origin of one's self-doubt or apprehension regarding potential failure. Frequently, it originates from a sequence of encounters we encountered during our formative years. It is highly uncommon for individuals to experience an abrupt onset of self-doubt while attempting to accomplish a task. It may have its origins in a personal setback experienced at a certain juncture in your life, when others conveyed their sense of disapproval towards you. You will be able to leverage the source of your self-doubt to your benefit once you have gained comprehension of its origins.

Throughout my entire life, I endured persistent self-doubt as a consequence of being brought up in an environment where I was consistently made to believe that I possessed weakness or limitations in certain aspects. I commenced harboring the notion of my own inadequacy, however, allow me to elucidate that when embarking upon the establishment of a home-based enterprise, one cannot afford to succumb to weakness or permit apprehensions to dictate their course of action. This is merely the approach that yielded success in my case, and it has the potential to be effective for you too. I harnessed all the skepticism that I knew was unrelated to my true identity, and employed it to propel my own growth and progress. I intended to refute the assertions of those who doubted my ability to succeed independently. I intended to demonstrate to them that I had overcome my previous vulnerability.

When initiating a task, it is imperative to reinforce the belief within oneself that it is indeed achievable. Indeed, it is a widely observed phenomenon that individuals, when adopting a belief or notion that they are incapable of accomplishing a certain task, exhibit a natural inclination to undertake any necessary actions that confirm the validity of their self-imposed limitation. The aforementioned statement holds true should you convince yourself of your capability to accomplish a task. If you find yourself grappling with persistent self-doubt, it may be prudent to explore the option of seeking professional counseling services.

9. Employ positive assertions to aid in the accomplishment of your necessary undertakings. If there is one factor that has greatly impacted my life, it is the adoption of positive affirmations and the unwavering belief in my ability to achieve all that I strive for. I embarked upon a process wherein I substituted all of my pessimistic thoughts with optimistic ones. I recommend that you attempt to experience them, at the very least. There is a plethora of freely accessible recordings available online, and should you make use of them for a span of a few weeks, I am confident that you will observe a considerable distinction.

The last point that I wish to address in this chapter pertains to impulsivity, indecisiveness, or immaturity. I possess a tendency towards impulsive behavior, and I am concurrently engaged in a multitude of hobbies. In the event that I were engaged in online work and happened upon a subject matter that piqued my curiosity or pertained to one of my personal pastimes, I would set aside my work obligations and allocate my attention towards the said hobby. As an illustration, I am among those individuals who actively seek out exceptional bargains and employ coupons as a means to obtain complimentary items. Therefore, in the event that I were to stumble upon a favorable transaction while browsing the internet, I would completely disregard my current activity, swiftly retrieve my coupons, and promptly make my way outdoors. I presume that immaturity played a significant role in this matter as well. Whilst I hold the perception that couponing holds significant importance in my life, serving as a means of substantial cost savings for my family, it does not take precedence over the most essential tasks that require my attention.

I could have easily documented the agreement, proceeded with my tasks, and subsequently made the purchases upon completing my work. This is the juncture at which we must all cultivate maturity, a matter of utmost significance for those engaged in remote work.

10. Maintain a comprehensive record of your priorities and carefully evaluate the

impact of your actions on those priorities. Contained within the pages of my scheduling journal lies a catalog of my foremost commitments. In moments where the lure of postponement threatens to divert my focus, I easily navigate to the rear section of my notebook and introspectively evaluate if such an inclination aligns with the advancement of my highest priorities. "Consider the practice of couponing as an illustration." I ponder whether engaging in that task will yield advantages for my family. The answer is yes. Will it result in cost savings for me? The answer is yes. Will my business derive any advantages from this? The response is negative. Subsequently, I must contemplate whether the task can be postponed, and undoubtedly the response is affirmative. Upon consistently deconstructing matters in this manner, the inclination to adopt such thinking patterns when faced with any decision will become innate.

Time Management

What does the concept of time management entail and how can it effectively propel individuals towards taking action, enhancing productivity, cultivating self-discipline, and ultimately achieving success? Allow us to present a narrative that effectively illustrates the concept of time management.

A professor presented three distinct assortments of pebbles, sizable rocks, and fine particles of sand to the class. He requests the assistance of a student volunteer to transfer the contents of all three trays into a receptacle. A student approaches the front of the classroom and diligently embarks on the assigned task. He commences with the particles of sand, subsequently progresses to pebbles, and ultimately endeavors to expel the larger stones. Nevertheless, to his profound disappointment, he is incapable of accommodating all of it within the container

Subsequently, the professor redirected his attention towards the class and declared that had the student adhered to the sequence of filling the container with rocks, followed by pebbles, and lastly sand, he would have successfully accommodated all the contents.

This exemplifies the precise workings of time management. It pertains to the arrangement of your stones, pebbles, and sand within the confines of a 24-hour time frame. Direct your attention to addressing the most demanding and considerable tasks initially, followed by the tasks of moderate complexity and lastly, the least complex ones. When prioritizing smaller tasks, individuals often demonstrate a propensity to excessively fixate upon them, thereby consuming an undue amount of time. Due to our propensity for excessive perfectionism and over-deliberation, we may allocate an unnecessarily greater amount of time to it. This allows limited time for tasks of medium to large scale.

Fundamentally, the paradigm of time management revolves around the meticulous organization, systematic scheduling, and strategic planning of one's existing temporal assets, with the ultimate objective being the attainment of optimal productivity. Should you fail to allocate a sufficient amount of time to attend to the significant matters, the minor tasks and trivialities will claim the entirety of your time.

The passage of time is invaluable, as it is irretrievable once it elapses. It is implausible to reverse the passage of time, regardless of one's strong desire to alter a certain event. Each individual is allocated an equal allocation of 24 hours within a day (unless one possess undisclosed technology or extraordinary capabilities). However, certain individuals effectively utilize their time, whereas others frequently express their lack of time for all activities.

How is it that certain individuals consistently manage to meet deadlines without difficulty, while others find it challenging to achieve a harmonious balance between work and leisure pursuits? Why is it that certain individuals are capable of not only fulfilling their obligations punctually but also finding pleasure in their recreational pursuits, while others struggle to meet their deadlines?

How is it that certain individuals consistently exhibit a propensity for proactively managing their workload, while others engage in frenetic, last-minute efforts to complete their tasks? The key lies in effectively managing one's time. The manner in which one maximizes the utilization of the allotted 24-hour period can significantly impact their level of productivity and efficiency.

Outlined below are a selection of highly-effective time management strategies that have the potential to significantly enhance productivity levels.

1. Create a morning routine. This statement bears no exaggeration, as the manner in which one commences their day significantly influences their productivity and value for the entire duration. It will determine the pace at which you will be able to accomplish your tasks throughout the day.

Avoid snoozing. While it may be tempting to press the snooze button and indulge in a few additional minutes of slumber, it is advisable to rise and commence one's activities. Remaining in bed will induce a sense of increased lethargy and drowsiness, in addition to the possibility of subsequently lapsing back into slumber. It will prove more challenging to rouse oneself after the sounding of the alarm.

Commence with a series of physical activities to experience a sense of revitalization and renewal. It will enhance neural activity within the brain and stimulate metabolic function. Even brief physical activity or spontaneous exercises can prove beneficial. Optimize your morning routine to establish the tone for the entirety of your day. I would strongly advise waking up before the other individuals in the household. This period presents a prime opportunity for you to accomplish tasks with utmost efficiency and effectiveness.

Additionally, this presents an opportune moment to strategically organize your daily agenda or engage in the mindful practices of yoga and meditation. Respond to electronic mail or devise a strategic agenda prior to the commencement of the day. If one finds oneself experiencing time constraints and an abundance of tasks scheduled throughout the day, it is advisable to enhance one's organizational skills. Generate a meticulously crafted and systematically arranged catalogue by directing your diligence and vitality towards paramount and time-sensitive assignments within the span of the day. Discern significant tasks from miscellaneous errands and arrange the latter in accordance with the former.

Please ascertain the three utmost essential tasks that necessitate completion throughout the course of the day. What are the things you really want to get done by the end of the day? Please prioritize these tasks. Everything else can wait. Do not endeavor to accommodate more tasks than you can manage within the given span of time. You will be stunned by how much progress you'll make with your time management simply by following this one tip.

2. Identify and eliminate activities that waste valuable time. Engage in this brief exercise to assess the allocation of a majority of your time. I referred to it as a daily assessment of time allocation. Do a seven-day audit of where you are spending your time. Document all information either by utilizing a mobile device, a physical notebook, or a designated journal. May I inquire as to your current activities? Divide it into intervals of 30 or 60 minutes. Have you been able to accomplish a significant

amount of tasks today? Has your time been utilized efficiently?

Have you engaged in any time-consuming or non-constructive pursuits? If one is employing the four-quadrant technique, it is highly recommended to classify one's activities in accordance with the four quadrants. At the conclusion of each week, compile all the numerical values. May I inquire about the principal allocation of your time? In which quadrant did the majority of your activities predominantly fall under? The outcomes might surprise you! Occasionally, we have a tendency to perceive ourselves as productive even when it is evident that we are not. We often deceive ourselves into believing that we are accomplishing a significant amount due to the practice of multitasking. Nevertheless, our cognitive capacity and effectiveness are compromised when engaged in multitasking excessively. Are you achieving the desired level of productivity and efficiency, or are you merely burdening yourself with an excessive workload?

Negative habits are the primary contributors to inefficiency, solely designed to diminish overall productivity. One of the most deleterious aspects of these distractions is that they cultivate a false perception of productivity. As an example, it is common for individuals to spend extended periods browsing the internet under the pretense of conducting research or seeking inspiration. Could you conceptualize the inefficient allocation of time that occurs when one spends hours on Instagram, Facebook, or Pinterest in an attempt to compile ideas? On the contrary, engage in a swift perusal and promptly return to your tasks.

Incorporate a timer if deemed necessary. I have found this to be an effective strategy for my needs. On every occasion when I feel tempted to engage in online research or seek inspiration during my designated work period, I conscientiously monitor the duration of my internet and social media browsing activities. Please initiate a timer for a duration of approximately 5 to 10 minutes. After the buzzing sound, your attention will be immediately redirected from leisurely activities such as browsing or indulging in creative thinking, towards focusing on your work. Likewise, exercise self-regulation in regard to the duration of your phone conversations.

One of the most significant misuses of time I have noticed is the constant monitoring and responding to emails throughout the course of the day. Our mailbox incessantly receives notifications throughout the day, leading us to feel an inclination to promptly attend to and respond to each email, thereby disrupting the flow and progress of our present activities. Avoid doing this. Alternatively, set aside a designated period for reviewing and responding to your emails, unless there is an imminent and critical need. Continuously evaluate whether the activities you are engaged in contribute any substantial value to your overall tasks or productivity.

Engaging in online networking platforms, indulging in mindless digital entertainment, excessively consuming series, and similar activities are all unproductive behaviors that drain your time and diminish your efficiency. Utilize your time effectively if you aspire to achieve your goals. The primary distinction between individuals who fail to succeed and those who achieve victory lies in the ability of the latter to exercise patience and focus on necessary tasks, all while keeping their sights firmly fixed on the broader perspective. Their primary focus lies in attaining long-term benefits, thereby propelling them towards their objectives through the efficient allocation of valuable temporal resources. They are rarely inclined to prioritize immediate gratification.

We all harbor a sense of admiration towards the affluent and accomplished, yet we are unable to summon the fortitude to endure the same hardships, surmount the challenges, or make the same sacrifices that ultimately lead to achieving a comparable level of success in life. In addition to numerous other factors that contribute to their success, some noteworthy elements include efficient time management, exercising delayed gratification, exercising self-discipline, the aptitude to overcome procrastination, and various other attributes. We are compelled to inquire as to why we have not achieved equal measures of success as those individuals whom we hold in high regard. Are you ready and willing to relinquish unproductive activities and detrimental habits? Are you fully equipped to exercise restraint in the same manner as they do? Are you ready to maximize your productivity and diligently strive each day to optimize the utilization of your invaluable time resources? Are you capable of forgoing immediate satisfaction in order to achieve long-term accomplishments? Deploy your time resources effectively if you genuinely aspire to achieve success.

Engaging in prolonged Netflix viewing or immersing oneself in virtual gaming activities without pursuing careers related to scriptwriting, movie making, or virtual game creation serves as a minimal contributor to productivity. Direct every minute towards maximizing your productivity. This has the potential to expedite your path towards success. Indeed, it is undeniable that on certain occasions, circumstances may become quite taxing. When one starts to experience a sensation of being inundated or daunted by the undertaking at hand, it is advisable to temporarily pause or indulge in a brief period of restorative slumber. Recenter yourself, and resume the task with revitalized verve and ardor.

Should you have perused Charles Duhigg's literary work entitled The Power of Habit, you would have encountered a discussion on keystone habits, which serve as the interconnecting elements of all other foundational habits. These foundational habits not only aid in cultivating additional constructive habits but they also facilitate the elimination of counterproductive habits. By placing our focus on keystone habits, we acquire the ability to effectively control our allocated time, thereby facilitating the establishment of habits pertaining to time management, avoidance of procrastination, and enhancement of productivity.

Promote the development and enhancement of the brain's opposite hemisphere. For instance, allocate your time to acquire competencies that lie outside of your usual realm of familiarity or exceed your own expectations. As an illustration, if one were to possess medical expertise, dedicating a portion of time to alleviating stress through the acquisition of dance skills would be advised. Likewise, a pianist holds the capacity to acquire expertise in the discipline of taekwondo. Engage in pursuits that lie outside your comfort zone in order to challenge your mind and cultivate the acquisition of novel abilities.

3. Get some inspiration when you are not feeling motivated. When you feel a decline in your motivation, you may turn to platforms such as YouTube, LinkedIn, or Ted Talks to invigorate your drive and enthusiasm. These resources can prove to be highly effective tools for regaining motivation and finding renewed inspiration. It proves to be arduous to accomplish tasks when the internal motivation is draining. Discover strategies for igniting your passion through focusing on inspirational material and actively searching for sources of motivation. Gaining inspiration and motivation from the accomplishments and strategies of others can reignite your own sense of drive and purpose.

Additionally, I appreciate the notion of acquiring a mentor who possesses the ability to provide guidance, foster accountability, and ensure adherence to the designated tasks. It is quite facile to become sidetracked and disheartened in the absence of proper guidance. Nevertheless, when there is someone we can depend on to offer guidance (especially if they have personally experienced hardship), we tend to exhibit increased initiative, accountability, and responsibility. It consistently instills us with motivation and inspiration, ensuring that we remain steadfast on the correct trajectory. Procure a mentor who possesses the ability to ensure your tasks and objectives remain in congruence.

4. Maximize the usage of your idle time. Utilize your idle time effectively. We have ample waiting periods that can be effectively utilized to enhance

productivity and optimize our available time. For instance, in locations such as the airport, the coffee shop while awaiting our order, the doctor's office, and so forth. Take advantage of this period of waiting by engaging in small tasks such as crafting a preliminary framework for a project, generating ideas, organizing events for the forthcoming day, correspondingly sending emails and messages, and similar activities. It is not feasible to undertake numerous tasks that require high focus and concentration during this period. Therefore, it is advisable to select an easier option that can significantly enhance the amount of time available for other activities. Significant progress in preliminary tasks can be accomplished during these brief intervals of time. It is widely recognized that a robust groundwork facilitates the construction of a sturdy edifice.

5. Partition a comprehensive task roster into four distinct quadrants. As you conclude each designated task, record it on the checklist to attain a deep sense of achievement, triumph, and contentment in successfully accomplishing each task, thereby fostering the motivation to undertake additional tasks.

Use your downtime judiciously. Throughout the course of the day, we have ample periods of downtime or idle time that can be effectively utilized for the purpose of creating your task list. Might I suggest making use of your travel time to efficiently strategize, arrange, and coordinate your tasks for the entire day? Additionally, the duration spent in transit may also be effectively utilized for engaging with audio books or podcasts.

It is advisable to refrain from dedicating all available leisure time solely to the task of arranging and scheduling one's day, as this approach may hinder the overall effectiveness of one's productivity and time management. If you possess approximately 15 to 20 minutes of spare time, allocate five minutes to effectively manage and structure the tasks for the day.

Also, ensure you maximize your weekends. I appear to be presenting myself as an excessively driven individual focused on productivity. Nevertheless, you will be astonished by the extent to which you can accomplish by effectively utilizing your weekends. There is a viral trend circulating on social media depicting a man energetically tossing documents into the air on Friday evening, while exclaiming an expression akin to "disregard, it is Friday." Subsequently, a subsequent image showcases the same individual dutifully gathering the scattered papers during the morning hours of the following Monday. Remarkably potent, in my opinion! Even a modicum of forethought and preliminary effort over the weekends can effectively alleviate the impending week's stress. It could encompass simplistic endeavors such as generating a preliminary version or strategizing one's weekly schedule.

Dedicate approximately 2-4 hours each day of the weekend to engaging in activities that foster productivity. You will still have ample time for relaxation and leisure activities over the weekends. Consider allocating tasks to the weekends and utilizing idle moments throughout the day, and observe the noticeable increase in your productivity.

Certain individuals who have achieved notable success are inclined to meticulously arrange their upcoming week's schedule a day prior to the commencement of the said week. This enables them to maintain their focus on their priorities, facilitating a smooth transition into the upcoming week. Transitioning abruptly from a state of relaxation over the weekend to a state of productivity on Monday can prove to be a formidable task. You can enhance the coherence and fluidity of the transition process by commencing it on Sunday itself.

Entering the work week with a well-defined plan enables one to concentrate on the most important tasks. By adequately preparing on Sundays, we can seamlessly shift our mindset from a leisurely weekend state to a focused and productive mindset for Monday mornings. Set aside a few minutes every Sunday to draft a comprehensive plan for the entire upcoming week. Mitigate the tendency to delay tasks by fragmenting weekly goals into smaller, daily objectives, thereby enabling the completion of subsequent tasks through a simple review of your comprehensive agenda.

It is important to bear in mind that your levels of energy, enthusiasm, and creativity tend to vary throughout the week. Assign low-demand and less critical tasks to Monday, or any other period when your motivation and vitality are comparatively diminished. Likewise, allocate tasks that require a demanding level of creativity and challenge to the days of Tuesday and Wednesday, as these are the days when your productivity is typically at its pinnacle. Arrange for meetings and brainstorming sessions to take place on Thursday, as this is when the team's energy levels start to decline. Utilize the day of Friday for fostering professional connections, conducting a comprehensive review of the week's activities, and strategizing for the future.

6. Create periodic reminders. To ensure you stay on track and optimize your time effectively, it is recommended that you establish periodic notifications, alarms, and deadline alerts on your electronic devices at regular intervals, rather than relying solely on the final deadline. Establishing timely reminders for intermediate deadlines enables one to effectively adhere to the ultimate deadline, thereby mitigating the tendency to procrastinate until the eleventh hour.

As an illustration, in the event that you possess a project requiring submission within the forthcoming 4 weeks, ensure to establish reminders not solely at the culmination of 28 days, but also on days 7, 12, 18, 24, and 28. This guarantees that you are making progress in line with the necessary tasks for project completion. You receive regular reminders about the task, enabling you to stay focused and avoid last-minute rushes to complete it within the deadline.

7. Rise early. Were you aware that individuals who are part of the 5 a.m. club include some of the most prosperous individuals globally? And here you are, peacefully slumbering and pondering the reasons behind your inability to achieve the opulence and triumph they witness. It pertains to the effective utilization of time, adherence to a structured routine, and conscious decision-making. You have agency over your actions, and they ultimately influence your likelihood of achievement.

In my opinion, my preferred method of time management would be waking up early and commencing tasks promptly. It confers a distinct advantage unrivaled by most other factors. It is noteworthy to mention here the renowned quote by Mark Twain. He stated, "Should the task of consuming a frog be assigned to you, it is advisable to undertake it as your topmost priority at the break of dawn." "If one is entrusted with the responsibility of consuming two amphibian specimens, it is prudent to commence with the consumption of the larger amphibious creature." This statement effectively encapsulates optimal strategies for efficient time management.

If you are apprehensive about the notion of accomplishing a substantial amount in a single day, initiate your activities at an early hour. Ensure all materials and preparations necessary for the task are completed the night before to minimize inefficiencies, such as indecision about where to commence.

For instance, consider a scenario where you are engrossed in the composition of a vital report, drawing upon the factual data and statistics that you have diligently gathered over a considerable period of time. Please ensure that all of your research is meticulously organized within a designated folder or document to facilitate convenient accessibility. Once all the necessary resources are at hand, initiating immediate action and gaining momentum becomes a straightforward task.

Nevertheless, should you expend valuable time attempting to determine the appropriate starting point, you inadvertently impede the progression of initiating and concluding the assignment. In the aforementioned illustration, commencing the task becomes more straightforward if all pertinent facts and statistics are readily accessible.

Likewise, in the event that you have a significant presentation or meeting planned for the following day, ensure to prepare your attire and all other necessary belongings on the preceding day to prevent any time wastage or unnecessary expenditure of energy in locating these items. A significant portion of our morning is dedicated to deliberating on our attire and crafting our appearance for the day. By ensuring that all preparations are completed in advance, one can devote their attention more efficiently to the primary task at hand.

Moreover, in the event that you have a multitude of commitments scheduled for the day, all of which hold great importance, it would be wise to commence with addressing the most demanding task. The purpose is to complete the task that requires the greatest amount of time and presents the greatest difficulty (recollecting the professor's analogy of sand, pebbles, and rock) by midday. Upon successful completion of a formidable task, one shall undoubtedly encounter an enhanced feeling of achievement. This will serve as a source of inspiration, prompting you to approach the remaining tasks with a proactive and assertive mindset.

When you are aware that you have ample remaining tasks to complete the following day or anticipate a lengthy work day, it is advisable to refrain from staying up late. Nothing obstructs your productivity and time management more severely than a lack of sufficient sleep. Retire to bed early, ensuring a tranquil undisturbed rest of approximately 8-9 hours, thereby waking up revitalized and prepared for the day ahead. Insufficient sleep may manifest as increased irritability, diminished energy levels, and impaired focus (reduced mental acuity and concentration).

One of the most detrimental actions you can take to impede your productivity and time management is to commence a day without any preconceived notions about where to initiate your tasks. Consider the scenario wherein one invests a considerable amount of time, approximately thirty minutes, deliberating on the most suitable starting point or determining the essential tasks that must be accomplished during the day. Such a period could have been utilized more effectively by initiating the day's obligations promptly and thereby finishing the tasks ahead of schedule. As a consequence of being delayed, you will have limited time available for organizing the forthcoming day's tasks. You are inadvertently trapped in a cycle of self-perpetuating negativity. Refrain from transitioning haphazardly from one task to another, thus squandering valuable time. Enhance your productivity by carefully designing your daily schedule in advance.

It is advisable to consistently ensure that the work desk is cleared at the end of the day, and to create a comprehensive agenda listing the tasks that must be accomplished the following day. It is recognized as the technique of decompression. Upon entering a desk that is tidier, better organized, and more aesthetically clean, you will encounter a feeling of optimism, revitalization, and an invigorating sense of newness. Punctually arrive at work, and diligently assemble the necessary materials required to commence the day productively. This particular suggestion has the potential to significantly influence your productivity throughout the day.

8. Optimize the utilization of time, work, and skills. Have you ever pondered upon the reasons behind certain individuals attaining extraordinary outcomes, while others merely endure despite having an equal allocation of 24 hours per day? Maximizing productivity through intelligent time management and skillful allocation of resources entails working smartly.

As an example, it should be noted that each individual possesses a total of 24 hours within a day, of which a maximum of 12-15 hours is typically available for constructive endeavors. If you dedicate yourself to working 15 hours per day, over the course of five days each week, you are effectively utilizing 75 hours of productive time, potentially leading to exhaustion and fatigue.

Now, let us juxtapose this with the utilization of individuals' time, exertion, and expertise. You have enlisted the services of three individuals, with each individual devoting 40 hours per week, resulting in a cumulative total of 120 hours per week. Do you perceive the disparity? Participating in a marathon may constrain your potential for personal development. There is a limit to what can be achieved through solitary effort.

Nevertheless, if one operates a relay, a multitude of tasks can be accomplished. By utilizing the resources of others, namely their time, effort, and energy, you can prevent yourself from experiencing burnout. Each individual is making a collective effort to enhance overall productivity, rather than relying solely on one person to handle all tasks. The significance of utilizing time, skills, and effort is widely recognized by individuals who have achieved exceptional success globally. They construct vast dominions by utilizing the time, endeavors, and skills of others.

Assign and contract out labor-intensive responsibilities. Remember Pareto's 80-20 rule? Merely a fraction of your efforts, namely 20 percent, are accountable for a substantial majority, precisely 80 percent, of the outcomes achieved. Pray tell, what prompts you to allocate the remaining 80 percent of your time towards an alternative pursuit? Wouldn't you be inclined to enhance your outcomes by dedicating additional time to the strategies that have evidently proven effective for you? Allocate duties and obligations that are consuming a substantial portion of your time.

Initially, it can prove challenging to delegate one's tasks to another individual. Nevertheless, in the event that you fail to provide adequate training and delegate tasks to individuals, you will find yourself undertaking the arduous task singlehandedly, thereby severely restricting the potential outcomes you may achieve. Assigning responsibilities and utilizing external resources can prove to be efficient means of time management. It alleviates your workload and enables you to direct your attention towards tasks that yield tangible outcomes. Furthermore, through intense concentration on a specific undertaking, you are effectively impeding the deceleration of your cognitive faculties. It is now widely acknowledged that multitasking is ill-advised. To enhance productivity and optimize personal efficiency, allocate additional time to activities that yield favorable outcomes, while entrusting labor-intensive tasks to appropriate individuals or teams. You have the option of delegating responsibilities to team members through comprehensive training and guidance, or alternatively, of engaging the services of proficient and seasoned freelancers. Employing individuals within the household may require an initial investment and training, yet it holds the potential for favorable outcomes over an extended period.

9. Make a routine. This particular matter appears logical and straightforward to me; however, it is somewhat amusing how numerous individuals overlook it. You are more likely to optimize your time by adhering to a well-defined schedule. In the absence of a predetermined daily timetable, the lack of time management will inevitably result in significant time wastage. Establish a well-defined timetable for

the various activities to be undertaken during the course of the day. This will ensure that you exert maximum effort to accomplish tasks. Organize each day with the same diligence as if you were orchestrating a significant occasion.

Here are several highly effective strategies for optimizing time management, enhancing productivity, reducing time wastage, efficiently utilizing available time resources, and breaking free from periods of inactivity.

15 Strategies That Will Enhance Your Workplace Productivity

By tidying your work area and allowing yourself an opportunity to express concerns, implementing these 15 straightforward behavioral adjustments can significantly enhance your daily productivity.

Individuals who successfully accomplish a significant amount on a daily basis are not endowed with superhuman abilities; rather, they have adeptly cultivated a few fundamental routines. Some aspects may pose difficulty to decipher: Maintain the orderliness of your workspace and strive to obtain approximately eight hours of sleep per night. Nonetheless, you may be astounded by other activities, such as engaging in a mid-day respite or expressing discontent.

Below, you will find a collection of 15 straightforward strategies to enhance the productivity of each day:

1. Clean up your desk.

Creativity may arise from disorder, however, it is likely that an office filled with litter is not conducive to productivity. According to Josh Davis, chief of research at the NeuroLeadership Institute and author of Two Awesome Hours, the purpose of studying is to make advancements and discoveries. Visible documentation facilitates the retention of pending tasks. A novel publication serves as a potent lure for the tendency to delay tasks. Irrespective of the potential absence of awareness regarding the perplexity, it detrimentally impacts your ability to concentrate.

According to a recent study published in Harvard Business Review, individuals who maintain an orderly work environment exhibit greater perseverance and experience reduced levels of depression and fatigue. The study revealed that a well-organized workspace enhances task engagement, leading to a significantly longer duration spent on a given assignment, up to one and a half times more.

According to Grace Chae, a professor at the Fox School of Business at Temple University and coauthor of the report, "Although finding comfort amidst chaos may be appealing, a disorderly environment can indeed serve as a significant hindrance."

2. Join the 20% cohort.

Irrespective of the hectic nature of your daily schedule, ensure that you deliberately carve out and rigorously allocate an hour and a half, which accounts for 20% of an eight-hour day, for the most essential tasks. "Even if one were to squander the remaining 80% of the day, considerable progress can still be made by allocating an hour and a half towards one's goals or priorities," remarks Kimberly Medlock, a productivity mentor based in Charlotte, North Carolina.

3. Work less.

Do you believe that by assuming additional hours, you can enhance your productivity? According to a recent report by John Pencavel, an esteemed Stanford educator, who analyzed data on workers during World War I, the outcome was directly proportional to the amount of time spent working, up until a maximum of 49 hours.

Furthermore, it experienced a gradual decrease in its rate of increase, and those individuals who dedicated 70 hours exhibited indistinguishable levels of productivity compared to those who worked 56 hours.

4. Quit phoning it in.

While you may acknowledge that you are not paying attention to your iPhone, it remains a significant source of distraction unless it is completely powered off.

In a study published this year in the Journal of Experimental Psychology: Human Perception and Performance, researchers from Florida State University discovered that even if individuals refrain from visually attending to their mobile phones when they receive notifications, the auditory alerts elicit cognitive distractions.

5. Attempt this email hack.

How Alexandra Samuel, the individual responsible for Work Smarter With Social Media, adeptly avoids becoming preoccupied during periods of anticipation for a crucial message.

1. Unearth the method of converting emails to text messages for your cellular provider through a concise query on Google.

2. By employing the aforementioned address, proceed to configure your email account such that it effectively diverts messages originating from a specific sender to your mobile device by means of content filtering (locate the "Rules" feature within the "Tools" menu in Outlook).

3. Temporarily disable receiving new emails and disregard incoming messages to focus on higher priority tasks, being confident that urgent messages will duly notify you.

6. Go massive on HVAS.

People tend to be more productive when they are engaged in tasks that flow smoothly, whereas activities that are challenging or arduous are likely to impede progress. If it should happen to be possible, endeavor to delegate tasks that appear laborious, and instead, prioritize "high value activities." According to Hillary Rettig, author of The Seven Secrets of the Prolific: The Definitive Guide to Overcoming Procrastination, Perfectionism, and Writer's Block, HVAs are aligned with your mission, leverage your strengths, and generate substantial impact or change.

Furthermore, they promote clarity and help in managing your schedule by delegating non-HVA tasks. This process also fosters a sense of community. Taking all factors into account, it is highly probable that they might belong to a different individual's highly valuable assets (HVAs)."

7. Meet smarter.

Three methodologies for maximizing the productivity of your gathering sessions:

i. Establishing a Formal Agreement

Many meetings lack a specific objective, however, it is crucial to ascertain your desired outcomes beforehand. According to Alan Eisner, a professor of management at Pace University's Lubin School of Business, it is advisable to limit the agenda to a maximum of three items in order to ensure that gatherings remain concise. After a period of time, share the minutes using your initiative, in order to inform everyone of their respective tasks."

ii. Expel distractions

Allocate extraneous musings to a designated mental space for reflection and analysis." "Participants may introduce ideas of personal significance but unrelated to the topic at hand," states Cary Greene, coauthor of Simple Sabotage: A Modern Field Manual for Detecting and Rooting Out Everyday Behaviors That Undermine Your Workplace. Instead of losing them, make sure to document them. Avoid allowing important issues to fall into a void by assigning follow-up actions at the conclusion of the meeting.

iii. Engage in the game of musical chairs.

Strolling meetings have gained traction in popularity, however, one can achieve similar benefits without venturing to the common areas. Please configure a timer for a duration of 30 to 45 minutes. When the alarm is activated, instruct everyone to stand and relocate.

According to work environment analyst Karissa Thacker, a beneficial practice is for the team to collectively stand up and engage in a brief physical activity to revitalize everyone. Regular physical activity provides various advantages, one of which is the improvement of our ability to focus."

8. Sleep on THE JOB.

While it might pose a challenge to convince your supervisor, a study conducted by researchers from the University of Michigan indicated that engaging in a daytime nap can effectively mitigate impulsive behavior and enhance one's capacity to endure frustrating circumstances. The findings also suggest that utilizing bulldozers in the workplace may enhance productivity.

9. Exercise caution regarding these factors that inhibit productivity.

The initial phase in avoiding distractions involves identifying them. According to a comprehensive study conducted by CareerBuilder in 2015, the following list comprises the primary five factors that negatively impact productivity in the workplace:

Mobile Phone/Messaging

Web

Gossip

Online social media

Email

Acquire the skill of slumber amidst the gusts of wind.

A compelling narrative on the value of proactivity": "I can rest assured when challenges arise.

In bygone years, there was a farm and cattle fair that once flourished in the rural expanse of England. Historically, this location functioned as a venue for displaying agricultural machinery, products, and livestock. Furthermore, farmers would employ farm laborers in that location.

Mr. Smith, an agricultural landowner situated along the coastal region of the North Antarctic Ocean, was in search of a male individual to be employed on his expansive farm. He was conducting interviews with prospective candidates. Upon learning about the location of his farm, the majority of the candidates exhibited a hesitancy to join him. The rationale behind this was that the farm's location was prone to frequent high wind storms, rendering it unattractive for laborers. He was captivated by the appearance of a contemplative young man who appeared to be around the age of sixteen. The young lad found himself faced with an unexpectedly direct inquiry from the stoic elderly farmer. What abilities do you possess?" The young boy retorted in a similar manner, "I have the skill to slumber when the wind doth blow.

Although he was dissatisfied with the response provided by the adolescent, there was an intriguing quality about the grey eyes of said individual that piqued his curiosity.

He once again approached the youth, posing the identical query, "Pray, what ability did you claim to possess?" Unfailingly, the youth echoed back the very same response, asserting, "I possess the capacity to slumber when the wind is afoot."

Mr. Smith remained thoroughly appalled by such a response and proceeded to explore different sections of the fair in order to encounter other prospective youths who might be interested in agricultural employment. Nonetheless, the impression of that particular answer lingered with him persistently, akin to an adhesive residue. Miraculously, his lower extremities propelled him towards the rendezvous with the resolute gaze of the young lad, who possessed a peculiar manner of communication.

Upon the farm help for the third instance, he bellowed, 'Could you kindly reiterate the abilities you claimed to possess?' Additionally, on the third occasion, the farmer received an identical response. . . . I am able to rest when the wind is in motion.

Driven by inquisitiveness regarding the individual and disheartened by the myriad of rejections from those unwilling to collaborate with him, Smith recruited the young man.

Late in the evening, several weeks afterwards, Farmer Smith was abruptly roused from his slumber well past midnight due to the presence of a possibly impending cyclonic disturbance. It appeared that strong gusts originating from the north rapidly intensified within a small span of time, posing a threat to the stability of the roof above him. The trees splintered and the sounds from outside thoroughly discomposed our companion's nervous system. The celerity with which he adorned his trousers was surpassed solely by the swiftness of the lightning as it fragmented the veil of darkness beyond. With one shoe only partially laced, he hurriedly ventured into the farmyard to assess the remaining intactness of the property. However, in such inclement weather, he realized that he would require the assistance of the recently employed young lad. He vocalized towards the upper floor of the attic where the individual in question was resting, yet the reaction was an audible manifestation of deep, nasal breathing. He ascended halfway up the staircase and repeated a thunderous noise, yet only a resonant snore reverberated in response. With great enthusiasm, he approached the young boy's bed and made every effort to rouse him, yet the youth remained undisturbed in slumber.

Filled with a combination of desperation and repugnance, he briskly exited into the premises of the farm. He initially made his way towards the bovine enclosure. Much to his delight, the dairy farmers were tranquilly ruminating, and the interior of their dwelling was as serene as it would be any other day. It did not require a significant amount of time for him to ascertain the manner in which the young lad rectified the imperfections in the bovine dwelling and restored the security mechanisms.

Despite the actions taking place that evening, he discovered an equivalent sense of peace within the pigpen.

He directed his attention towards the haystack. As he navigated through the veil of darkness, it took him only a brief moment to reestablish the observance of the young individual possessing unwavering, gray eyes. Every few feet on that feed stack wires had been thrown with weight on each side. Through the implementation of this structure, all elements were harmoniously regulated.

Smith was astounded by the revelations that he experienced within a brief duration on that tumultuous night. He dropped his head. The sentiments of despair and repulsion gave way to a smile adorning his countenance. He was compelled to recall an amusingly peculiar response provided by the boy several weeks prior: 'I can slumber in the face of turbulent gusts.' It was only in the present moment that Smith comprehended the profound significance and weightiness concealed within the words.

He privately reflected, "Never before have I encountered such a genuinely supportive and proactive assistant."

Being proactive allows for efficient time management and serves as a preemptive measure to mitigate potential issues by ensuring that we are adequately prepared to address them in advance.

Examining the potential consequences of the present moment is the most effective approach to prevent future disorder. Entrepreneurs who display a proactive approach are at lower risk of being taken by surprise, thereby enabling them to effectively manage risk and transform potentialities into favorable outcomes instead of obstacles.

Save Time and Money. Proactive measures have proven to be more effective than reactive solutions, as strategic investment and readiness can yield significant savings in mitigating potential losses.

In Stephen Covey's renowned literary work, "The 7 Habits of Highly Effective People," the first habit delineated is that of proactivity. Covey eloquently defines this concept as assuming personal accountability and adopting a solution-oriented mindset. Promote this practice within the professional environment by requesting employees to submit any issues along with a proposed resolution.

Technique 8 - Implement Regularly Timed Intervals of Rest

Burnout represents the most detrimental outcome for individuals who consistently invest significant effort and dedication in their work. This phenomenon arises when individuals exert excessive levels of effort and subsequently experience a decline in performance, characterized by either pronounced fatigue or subpar output. The majority of individuals would concur that a gradual and consistent approach to accomplishing objectives is significantly more viable, not only to maintain motivation but also for the preservation of one's health.

In order to mitigate burnout, individuals must consistently prioritize the allocation of brief periods of rest between each sequential task. In a customary professional environment, employees are allocated a 15-minute interval amidst two hours of work, accompanied by a single allocated lunch break during a cumulative period of eight hours. Grant yourself the opportunity to recharge and rejuvenate by indulging in this pause. If you are engaged in remote work, it is advisable to plan your intervals by employing an alarm or timer.

Engaging in intermittent periods of rest can effectively enhance one's ability to concentrate and generate improved levels of productivity subsequently. As an example, you may elect to rise and move around briefly to prevent later distractions caused by discomfort in the buttocks. An alternative approach would be to adopt a seated or reclined position and engage in a session of meditation, which can effectively facilitate mental clarity and enhance your ability to make sound judgments.

I trust that you are finding this book to be enjoyable thus far. It is crucial that you incorporate every skill you possess into your daily routines.

I trust that you are finding satisfaction in your experience with this eBook. I trust that you are diligently documenting all the information you are acquiring. If you have found the content thus far to your satisfaction, we would greatly appreciate it if you could take a moment to share your thoughts and graciously provide us with a review, including a few words of praise.

Kindly navigate to the designated area on amazon.com in order to provide your valued feedback and review.

Enhance Your Concentration through Skill 9

Attaining a high level of concentration does not occur instantaneously. It is an aptitude that necessitates consistent practice. The heightened level of concentration you maintain directly correlates to the pace at which you complete your tasks and consequently reduces any inefficiency caused due to time wastage.

In order to enhance your concentration, it is imperative to identify a tranquil environment where you can direct your attention. Certain individuals prefer to center their attention on their academic pursuits within the serene atmosphere of a quaint café, whereas others opt to establish a designated workspace within the confines of their own residence, shielding themselves from potential disturbances such as the presence of a television.

Additionally, it is imperative to determine the duration of time required for you to maintain focused attention on a given task. Commence your task immediately after initiating a systematic measurement using a chronometer. Once you begin to experience fatigue and susceptibility to distraction, promptly activate the stopwatch and meticulously record your threshold. Strive to continuously extend the duration of that constraint.

Furthermore, it is imperative that you exert conscious effort in managing your interactions with individuals. A communication or contact initiated by a close associate can still disrupt your focus, thus it is advisable to inform them that you are unavailable during specific intervals of the day. Alternatively, please activate the airplane mode on your mobile device.

I'm Not Sure Where To Begin.

Lacking the knowledge of where to begin can also be a legitimate cause for engaging in procrastination. Fundamentally, individuals experience such a degree of apprehension regarding their obligations that it ultimately paralyzes them into inaction. As an illustration, you are required to undertake the task of cleaning the premises, albeit, it has been previously deferred to such an extent that the accumulation of dirt has reached an unimaginable degree. If such is the scenario, it is highly probable that you will refrain from taking any measures to tidy the premises.

In certain scenarios, individuals may encounter difficulties initiating a task due to a lack of requisite expertise. This is true when it comes to homework, papers, or any other task that feels new to you.

If the task appears daunting and is thus contributing to procrastination, the following strategies are recommended for addressing the issue:

Conduct an Initial Examination

This deduction appears to be quite evident – however, a scarce number of individuals choose to pursue this alternative. You may find it astonishing how valuable the internet can be in offering supplementary assistance for unfamiliar subjects. There are sources available that provide comprehensive visual instructions, enabling you to replicate their actions precisely. In addition, perusing instructional videos available on the YouTube platform may prove beneficial. It is advantageous to store these articles and videos in your online archive. This way, when you find yourself leisurely lounging on your bed, you can readily access them on your mobile device and engage in reading. In this manner, you are still actively contributing to the accomplishment of your obligations, even if you haven't commenced the actual execution yet.

A noteworthy aspect of perusing these instructional videos and articles is that they incite a desire within oneself to experiment with the suggested techniques. On occasion, gaining insights into the workflow and envisioning the expected outcome can be sufficient to enhance one's time management skills.

Divide It

This matter has already been deliberated upon in a preceding section. If you perceive the task to be excessively demanding, it may be advantageous to break it down into more manageable segments to alleviate any feelings of being overwhelmed. For instance, in the event that all the rooms in the house are in a state of disarray, it may be advantageous to undertake the task of tidying them up individually, room by room. By doing so, you can direct your attention solely to a specific area of the house, without the need to be concerned about the remaining portions of the room. Upon completion, you may proceed to attend to another room and continue in this manner until all tasks are completed.

Commence with the things you enjoy.

Suppose that all of your household tasks have accumulated. The laundry requires attention, the sink is burdened with unwashed dishes, and the floor is laden with copious amounts of dog hair brought about by your Siberian Husky. You may be experiencing a sense of being inundated and uncertain about where to commence – yet, you are cognizant of the imperative nature of initiating action in some capacity.

If you choose to do so, why not commence in a location that you genuinely enjoy? Certainly, it is generally known that the majority of individuals do not derive pleasure from engaging in household tasks. However, it is noteworthy that certain domestic duties are preferred by individuals relative to others. You may find it agreeable to undertake the task of dishwashing, or alternatively, if it aligns with your preference, you might be inclined towards the activity of ironing garments. Irrespective of the nature of the task, initiate your daunting undertaking with the aforementioned one and progress accordingly. In regards to domestic chores, one will discover that they have the potential to operate akin to an avalanche. After accomplishing a task proficiently, subsequent endeavors tend to be facilitated.

Chapter 1: Recognizing Activities That Consume Valuable Time

Time Killers

The majority of individuals are unaware of their tendency to squander time, yet it remains a fact. It is possible that you perceive yourself as lacking sufficient time. Perhaps you believe that the workload is simply overwhelming.

Alternatively, it could be a combination of the two possibilities. Whilst it may indeed be accurate that you have an excess of obligations, it is essential to acknowledge that individuals tend to engage in activities that consume their valuable time on a routine basis.

Individuals often fail to comprehend the extent to which they squander valuable time in their daily routines. Frequently, it is the seemingly uncomplicated tasks, which we typically perceive as taking only a moment, that can accumulate rapidly. Moreover, throughout the span of a single day, this can accumulate into several hours of unproductive time that cannot be retrieved. To utilize your time more efficiently, it is essential to first identify and discern your areas of weakness.

By devoting a day exclusively to documenting your activities, it won't be long before patterns indicative of the areas of concern become apparent. You might promptly begin to observe/acknowledge them. Simply possessing awareness is the initial stride in the endeavor to discern the elements that squander your valuable time.

At times, we all fall victim to distractions that consume our time. These factors result in tardiness, hinder the achievement of objectives, impede task completion, and disrupt time management. Naturally, one desires to accomplish their tasks efficiently, and if they possess the determination and resolve, they must be mindful of how their time is allocated. It can encompass a myriad of possibilities. Presented herewith are illustrative instances of activities that could potentially impede productive use of time.

Excessive engagement in online social networking platforms. For instance, notable examples include social media platforms such as Facebook, Twitter, Tumblr, Instagram, as well as online dating websites. You may simply wish to perform a brief inspection to ascertain the current situation, but subsequently find yourself engrossed in watching videos or perusing content for a duration of one hour. Occasionally, even the most exceptional individuals experience such occurrences. However, if you possess the knowledge or consciousness, you have the ability to cease this practice. Alternatively, you may incorporate it into your personal schedule.

Procrastinating. (This is one of the most significant sources of wasted time.) Delaying tasks due to personal preference and assuming they can be completed at a later time will not result in improved outcomes upon their eventual completion. It has the potential to exacerbate the situation due to the extensive contemplation time you have experienced. Please proceed and conclude the task promptly.

Overbooking yourself. It is not possible for an individual to be present in multiple places simultaneously. One is not always required to feel obliged to comply with others' requests. Always prioritize and ensure you allocate the necessary time for your tasks. One must come to terms with the reality that individuals will perpetually hold expectations, and it is permissible to occasionally disappoint them.

Watching too much TV. Set a specified duration for yourself. Typically, dedicating one hour per day is sufficient for individuals to decompress and de-stress while watching television. Furthermore, one can engage in attending to minor tasks during intermissions. You have the option to tidy up the kitchen by sweeping, engage in physical activity by taking the dog for a stroll, or even incorporate some exercise into your routine. Do not allow yourself to become overly engrossed in streaming services such as Netflix or Hulu. It is remarkably convenient to continuously select the subsequent episode, inadvertently resulting in the passage of a significant portion of the day.

Devoting excessive amounts of time to the contemplation of one's mobile device. (The majority of individuals are culpable of this) The cellular phone serves as a commendable apparatus, however, it is imperative to exercise caution and avoid becoming excessively reliant on it. If an individual is unable to refrain from using their cell phone for even an hour, it suggests that they are devoting an excessive amount of time to it.

Fretting over matters beyond your ability to alter or regulate. If one is unable to exert any influence towards altering a given circumstance, it is best to abstain from expending considerable mental energy in unnecessary distress. It will deplete your energy and impede your ability to accomplish essential tasks.

Regarding the act of watching television or engaging in social media, it is deemed acceptable to partake in these activities within reasonable limits. Allocate a specific duration for the accomplishment of these tasks. By consistently performing that action rather than sporadically checking, you will be able to save a significant amount of time.

There exist a multitude of factors that contribute to the squandering of our time. The factors that consume our time vary for each individual, yet the result remains consistent. As a result of our persistent inability to complete essential tasks, we find ourselves frequently overwhelmed with excessive workloads and heightened levels of stress, yet regrettably lacking tangible accomplishments. When one exhibits a propensity to leave tasks unfinished, it engenders heightened levels of stress and squanders additional time. It constitutes a detrimental cycle, yet you hold the authority to terminate it. The present moment presents an opportune occasion for you to reclaim control over your life and the utilization of your time.

You can be productive and successful. The initial stage entails the identification of activities that consume your time excessively, followed by the implementation of measures to eliminate them.

Motivate yourself intrinsically

Motivation is a concept that diverse individuals perceive and interpret in distinct manners.

Assuming that the objective you have in mind is to reduce your body weight. When one reflects on motivation, it conjures images of the delightful indulgence in a delectable serving of cookies and cream-flavored ice cream that awaits at the culmination of a week dedicated to consuming salads.

Suppose that your objective entails diligently pursuing career advancement, it is likely that you are leveraging your aspiration for financial prosperity and material possessions as a means to cultivate unwavering commitment and motivation, thereby circumventing any inclination towards procrastination and consistently maintaining your industriousness.

It is possible that neither of these options align with your objective. Perhaps your objective is something altogether dissimilar.

I urge you to pause and reflect upon the driving forces that you employ to pursue your ultimate objective.

Does it pertain to a tangible entity, such as a material possession, a substantive prize such as sustenance, currency, apparel, and the like?

If such is the case, a reevaluation of your approaches may be prudent.

To commence our discussion, let us direct our attention towards extrinsic motivation. The aforementioned description pertains to extrinsic motivation, which can be defined as the motivation derived from the anticipation or aspiration for a tangible reward.

A study carried out by Sam Glucksberg, a researcher in the field, involved the participation of two distinct groups who were presented with a task and tasked with resolving it. The participants in one group were provided with an incentive, whereas the participants in the other group did not receive any form of reward.

It was determined that, on average, the individuals comprising the group presented with incentives exhibited a three and a half minute longer duration in comparison to the group lacking any form of offer.

It's surprising, I know. One might expect that the anticipation of a reward would enhance one's enthusiasm and speed, but it appears to have the opposite effect. It hampers cognitive processes, stifles innovative thinking, and incapacitates productive endeavors.

An additional demonstration of this was conducted by economist Dan Ariely and his colleagues. They assembled a group of university students and engaged them in a series of games revolving around creativity and concentration. The students were incentivized based on their performance, ranging from modest to substantial rewards. It was determined that in cases where the game necessitated skills beyond basic mechanics, a higher incentive resulted in diminished performance.

Economists at the London School of Economics (LSE) conducted a comprehensive analysis of various strategies implemented by businesses, which entailed the adoption of a 'pay for performance' model. Their research unequivocally ascertained that the provision of incentives under such schemes leads to an adverse influence on overall performance outcomes.

Consequently, what implications does that carry for you?

It indicates that in order to summon self-motivation and overcome procrastination, it is imperative to refrain from undertaking such endeavors solely for the sake of attaining tangible rewards.

Instead, redirect your attention towards motivating yourself by considering how this undertaking will enhance your skills, elevate your personal growth, and so forth. This phenomenon is commonly referred to as intrinsic motivation, which has proven to be considerably more efficient in enhancing productivity and facilitating the adherence to one's objectives.

Now, you have been enlightened about the optimal approach to self-motivation— a crucial aspect for overcoming procrastination tendencies and increasing overall productivity.

Let us proceed to the subsequent chapter, wherein a more comprehensive discussion on procrastination awaits, along with strategies to overcome it.

www.ingramcontent.com/pod-product-compliance
Lightning Source LLC
Chambersburg PA
CBHW050352120526
44590CB00015B/1665